LEWIS CARROLL

The British Council

PUBLISHED BY
The British Council
10 Spring Gardens London SW1 2BN

EXHIBITION CURATED BY
Roger Taylor

PUBLICATION EDITED BY
Charlotte Byrne

PHOTOGRAPHY EXHIBITION ORGANIZED BY
Brett Rogers and Sean Williams,
Visual Arts Department,
The British Council

DESIGNED AND TYPESET BY
Orna Frommer-Dawson,
John and Orna Designs, London

PRINTED BY
Clifford Press Ltd, Coventry

ISBN 0 86355 377x

SPECIAL MENTION AND THANKS TO
Janet McMullin,
Christ Church Library, Oxford

Amanda Nevill,
The National Museum of Photography,
Film & Television, Bradford

Roy Flukinger and David Coleman,
Harry Ransom Humanities Research
Center, The University of Texas
at Austin

Pierre Apraxine and Maria Umalli,
Gilman Paper Company Collection,
New York

William Joyce, John Bidwell and
Peter Bunnell, Princeton University,
Princeton

Elizabeth Fuller & Jason A. Staloff,
The Rosenbach Museum &
Library, Philadelphia

Ken Scott, Warrington Museum

And special thanks to
Edward Wakeling for sharing his
knowledge so generously on the subject
matter and chronology of
Charles Dodgson's photography.

CONTENTS

FOREWORD

page 5

ESSAYS

'NONSENSE IS REBELLION': THE CHILDSPLAY OF LEWIS CARROLL

BY MARINA WARNER

page 7

'SOME OTHER OCCUPATION':

LEWIS CARROLL AND PHOTOGRAPHY

BY ROGER TAYLOR

page 27

LEWIS CARROLL

BY MICHAEL BAKEWELL

page 39

PLATES

page 47

LEWIS CARROLL — FURTHER SELECTED READING

page 72

LIST OF WORKS

page 73

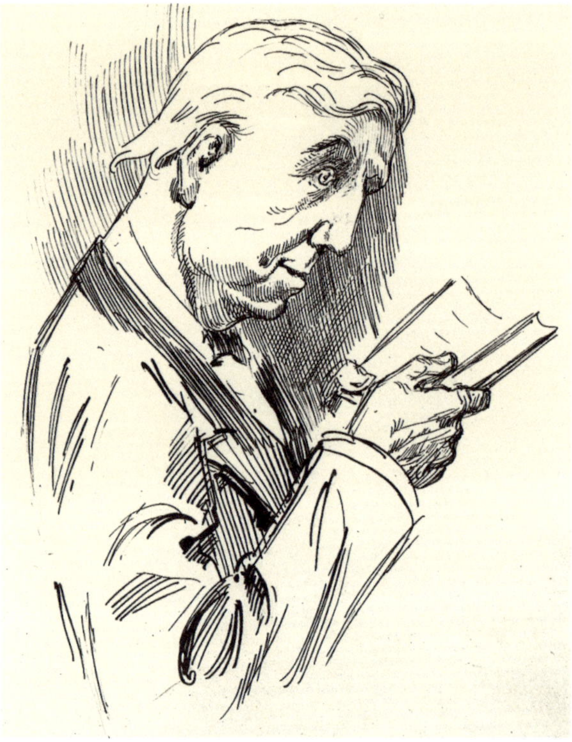

Pen and ink cartoon of Lewis Carroll by Harry Furniss

As we near the end of the twentieth-century there is in some respects no figure more contemporary than the Victorian novelist and mathematician Lewis Carroll. Across one hundred years his appeal is stronger than ever. Innately English, Carroll crosses cultural frontiers with ease, making people laugh and dream and occasionally cry whether or not they read his original language or know how innovative were his camera techniques.

Part of this universal fascination is with Carroll the man. Vulnerable in his sexuality, wrestling with the dilemmas of being both an artist and a professional man, we interpret him today with particular sympathy, as though he anticipated the anguishes and sensibility of our time. In uniting the worlds of the imagination and logic he implicitly looks forward to the magic realism, science fiction and fantasies of modern literature. Yet in so many respects, as some of the poses of his photographs demonstrate, he remains quintessentially Victorian. He is often described as some kind of zany one-off interloper amid the confident proprieties of the late nineteenth-century. In truth he was full of the self-doubt, ambitious imaginings and intellectual uncertainties which we conventionally associate with the century after him, but which were really as much part of the psychological composition of his own time.

The manner in which Lewis Carroll explores issues of personal identity through concepts of multiple selves is only now beginning to be fully understood. What has, of course, been appreciated from the start is his extraordinary ability to empathise with children and adults alike. His Alice books are read all over the world in every age group. People respond to the vividness and humour of his imagination. They delight in his insatiable curiosity, his mad logic, his riddles, his charm, his moments of brutality, his sense of life poised perpetually on the edge of a chasm.

Creating these exhibitions for the centenary of Lewis Carroll's death has not been without its challenges to those involved, all of whom, however, have had fun with the project. Quite simply, Carroll keeps us smiling. For this reason the collaboration between the Literature and Visual Arts departments of the British Council has been very happy, the first we hope of many such partnerships.

For the literary exhibition organized by the Literature Department, we are indebted to Carroll's biographer Michael Bakewell, who has assiduously compressed a complex life into a manageable format, illustrated with wit and originality. We are equally grateful to Roger Taylor, photographic historian and curator, for selecting on behalf of the Visual Arts Department the photographic material, some hitherto unpublished. We also thank Marina Warner for her spirited and perceptive introduction to this publication.

Further thanks must be expressed to Charlotte Byrne, Hilary Jenkins and Sean Williams of the British Council for their crucial roles in the creation of the exhibitions, and of course to all those who have lent visual material or given permission for its reproduction.

ALASTAIR NIVEN
Head of Literature, The British Council

BRETT ROGERS
Head of Exhibitions, Visual Arts, The British Council

'NONSENSE IS REBELLION': THE CHILDSPLAY OF LEWIS CARROLL

BY MARINA WARNER

In 1849, the year he left school, Lewis Carroll wrote and illustrated a miscellany magazine. A comical, high-spirited collection of poems, stories and cuttings, it was compiled for his family's amusement, and he called it *The Rectory Umbrella* after a favourite tree in their garden at Croft. The frontispiece shows a bearded old man, beaming as fairies fly under the shelter of his umbrella.[1] They are bringing cradle blessings, labelled 'Good Humour', 'Knowledge', 'Mirth', and 'Cheerfulness' – among other boons. Above them, comical grimacing goblins are hurling rocks – these are 'Woe', 'Spite', 'Gloom', 'Crossness', 'Ennui' and 'Alloverishness' (presumably from the woeful cry, 'It's all over.') Most tellingly of all, the umbrella that is shielding the good sprites has written between its spokes, 'Jokes', 'Riddles', 'Poetry', 'Tales', and in the centre, 'Fun'. Even as a schoolboy, Lewis Carroll interposed his inventive brand of fun between himself and unhappiness; he saw humour as somewhere above all to shelter; it was fun, but it also had a purpose, and that purpose was intertwined with children and a child's way of being.

1. Lewis Carroll, *The Rectory Umbrella & Mischmasch* (London, 1932), f.p. 1.

2. Lewis Carroll, *Looking-Glass Letters*, ed. Thomas Hinde, (London, 1991), p. 21.

Within the family circle, he cast himself as an entertainer; the family was so numerous that they made up a party all to themselves. In one of the few surviving letters written home from school to his sister Elizabeth, the young Charles expresses an exile's frustration in a spate of questions: '...Are my two pictures of cricketing framed yet? ...Are the mats finished?... Is Skeffington's [his brother] ship finished?... Has Fanny found any new flowers?... Mary any new pictures to paint?...' But in the midst of this picture of tasks, pastimes and hobbies, he puts another, highly revealing question, 'Have you any more babies to nurse?'[2] He had five younger sisters, and three younger brothers and none of them was a twin, so that over his childhood, another baby was born every year or so. He remained close to his sisters all his life, moved them to Guildford, Surrey, after their father's death, and provided for them from his earnings, since only one of them married. He also had three maiden aunts, and although not enough material survives to uncover the lives of this prolific sorority, the overwhelming presence of spinsters in his personal life matches the writings' interest in singularity – literally and metaphorically.

There are scarcely any married people of any consequence in the *Alice* books, with the exception of the three royal couples – the King and Queen of Hearts in *Alice's Adventures in Wonderland* and the Red and White Kings and Queens in *Through the Looking-Glass* – and in every case, the women eclipse their vacillating spouses. The triple plot of *The Story of Sylvie and Bruno* does include a romance, but it is awkwardly handled. The best of Carroll's writings do not even set up enduring friendships. Alice continues on her journey alone, and her encounter with the White Knight, which is coloured by a certain poignant nostalgia for a lost intimacy, revealingly assumes that they will never meet again. Though *The Rectory Umbrella* fended off 'Alloverishness', it did not admit the possibilities of mutual attachment or tackle ideas of engagement and love in the way that George MacDonald does in his children's books, through his variations on medieval quests and the chivalrous figure of Curdie, his hero.[3] MacDonald was a friend of Lewis Carroll, after they met at a doctor's in Hastings; they were coincidentally both consulting him for a cure for their stammers (!). The MacDonalds enthusiastically encouraged Lewis Carroll to publish *Alice in Wonderland*, and structural and thematic coincidences abound between MacDonald's *Phantastes* (1858) and the *Alice* books.[4] Carroll

3. See George MacDonald, *At the Back of the North Wind* (1871) and *The Princess and the Goblin* (1872).

4. See John Docherty, *The Literary Products of the Lewis Carroll-George MacDonald Friendship* (Lewiston, Queenston, Lampeter, 1995).

also took eloquent photographs of the MacDonald daughters, (see plates page 57 and 63) some of them showing the little girls dreaming. But, while the Scottish fairy-tale writer may have profoundly influenced Carroll's metaphysics of innocence, and confirmed his investment in the child as hero, Carroll did not – perhaps could not? – absorb his commitment to love as a motive force.

It might be fruitful to speculate that as a boy, Lewis Carroll was eroticized to his particular form of singularity by the many very young girls surrounding him at home. He placed himself in charge of the fun there, just as he did later with his 'child-friends'. When Henry Liddell arrived at the Deanery, Christ Church, with his wife and their four children (more were on the way), they offered a kind of mirror image of Carroll's own family, and of his own sisters. Alice, who was to inspire the famous books, was three when she arrived in Oxford, the second of the Liddell daughters, but she did not emerge as his best loved 'child-friend' immediately, not until Carroll had adopted himself into the whole family of the young Liddells – photographing them, play-acting with them, arranging no end of treats and outings and surprises.

When there are couples in the *Alice* books, they tend to be *doppelgängers*, like the Red Queen and the White Queen and Tweedledum and Tweedledee, or they represent paired contrasts, like the Gryphon and the Mock Turtle, the Walrus and the Carpenter, the Mad Hatter and the Dormouse, and, again and again, Alice engaging her 'adventure': the Rabbit, Humpty Dumpty, the Caterpillar, the Cheshire Cat. Working in binary variations, Carroll generates a sequence of doubles for himself as well as for Alice. He writes of Alice at the beginning of

Wonderland, 'This curious child was very fond of pretending to be two people...'[5] Inside his pseudonym, he was not merely pretending to be two people in order to dialogue with himself, like Alice. Some of the doubles function as complementary mirror selves, and some as oppositional alter egos, or anti-selves. In one sense there can be no exploration of union or engagement in the *Alice* stories because Carroll's phantasms are not separate enough to be Others, in the sense of other people, however dazzlingly realized and sharply drawn they are. 'The Snark *was* a Boojum, you see' was the line that famously floated into Lewis Carroll's head, and inspired the whole epic farrago of inventive nonsense, *The Hunting of the Snark: An Agony in Eight Fits*. The single line encapsulates Dodgson/Carroll's sense of concealed and interfused riddling and contrary identities within one entity.

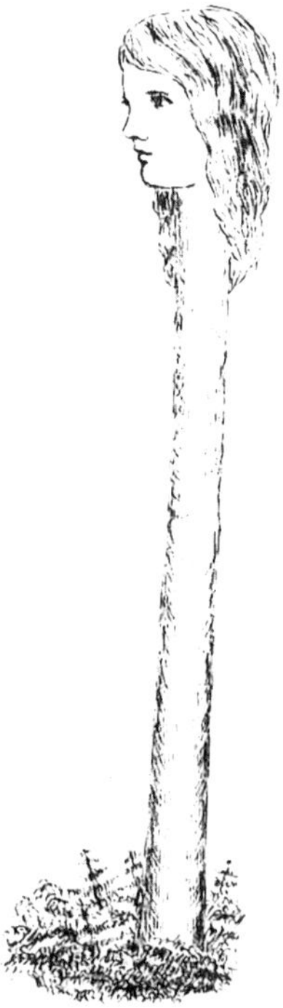

[Figure 1]
Illustration by Lewis Carroll from *Alice's Adventures Under Ground*

Alice experiences all kinds of changes, outside and in, from the moment she falls down the rabbit-hole and grows tall and short and tall and short. Her later transformations even hint at the monstrous (at the Boojum inside *her*), when she nibbles at the Caterpillar's mushroom and shape-shifts, now shrinking till her chin hits the ground, now growing 'an immense length of neck': 'she was delighted to find that her neck would bend about easily in any direction, like a serpent. She had just succeeded in curving it down into a graceful zig-zag...' when a pigeon attacks her:

'Serpent!' screamed the Pigeon.
'I'm *not* a serpent!' said Alice...[6]

Carroll illustrated the episode with two drawings of this

5. Lewis Carroll, *Alice's Adventures in Wonderland* [Miniature Edition, 1907] (London, 1940), p. 13.

6. Carroll, *Wonderland*, p. 72-3.

metamorphosed Alice in the manuscript version; they are more awkward than his usual illustrations, perhaps on account of the patent phallic character of his fantasy. Tenniel did not reinterpret them.[7]

The *Alice* books are tales of strictly personal quests, through the permutations of possibility that are – almost – infinite. The modernity of their magic – which has meant they have far outshone George MacDonald's books, for example, in worldwide popularity – consists of this polyvalent and solipsistic character of the Carrollian idea of the individual. 'I wonder if I've been changed in the night?' Alice muses. 'Let me think: *was* I the same when I got up this morning? I almost think I can remember feeling a little different. But if I'm not the same, the next question is, Who in the world am I? Ah, *that's* the great puzzle!'[8] This is indeed the great puzzle that has animated post-Victorian (and post-Christian) philosophy since Kant, and Carroll's signal contribution was to place, at the core of the self, the experiences of fantasy and imagination. His conception of the inner 'wonderland' and 'looking-glass country' enriched and stretched empiricism, but at the same time profoundly upset its assumptions, anticipating the destabilizing of unitary personality in the most adventurous philosophers today, like Richard Rorty and Ian Hacking.[9]

The enigma of Carroll is insoluble: how does the stiff, pedantic, Tory don, High Churchman and lacklustre lecturer in mathematics fit with the lightfooted, breezy, amiable, humorous inventor of stories, games, jokes, puzzles and treats? His biographers have attempted to answer the riddle. Morton Cohen emphasizes his life beyond *Alice* and the well-roundedness of his personality with such

7. Lewis Carroll, *Alice's Adventures Under Ground* (facsimile manuscript, London, 1995), no pp.

8. Carroll, *Wonderland* p. 19.

9. See for example, Ian Hacking, *Rewriting the Soul, Multiple Personality and the Sciences of Memory*, (Princeton, 1995).

anxiety that he unfortunately almost manages to make Carroll dull.[10] Michael Bakewell, with a more sensitive ear for the English nuances of Carroll's background, education and opinions, draws his subject as a historically-recognizable type, a pernickety bachelor don, a Victorian scientist-inventor and favourite uncle, sometimes naively starstruck in his pursuit of acquaintances (like Tennyson), and a doughty and innovatory thinker on a range of chosen causes, including proportional representation and the fairness of tennis tournaments.[11] His portrait shows Lewis Carroll vividly in his times and history.

But Carroll's inner processes necessarily elude, since Lewis Carroll never revealed himself, never apologized, never explained. 'Almost none of Carroll/Dodgson's surviving writing bears the imprint of ordinary, subjective first-person experience –' writes Hugh Haughton. 'Not even his letters and diaries, where we might expect to find it.'[12] Carroll's opaque, plural identity replicates the view of character in the *Alice* books as labile and polymorphous, although Carroll himself presented in so many ways a most conventional, and indeed stuffy, face to the world. But maybe this Snark *was* a Boojum, but did not want to own it himself, or anyone else to know it either.

Though Lewis Carroll did not reflect on his role and its history, he played the jester in Victorian society just as the Fool in the medieval and Renaissance court mimicked and mocked authority, convention – and the individuals invested with their power. The anthropologist Mary Douglas has pointed out, in her essay on Humour, 'The joke works only when it mirrors social forms; it exists by virtue of its congruence with the social structure.'[13] She goes on to discuss the 'joker', a traditional figure among certain African tribes, who enjoys

10. Morton N. Cohen, *Lewis Carroll: A Biography* (London, 1996); see Marina Warner, review in *London Review of Books* 18, 1, 4 January 1996.

11. Michael Bakewell, *Lewis Carroll: A Biography* (London, 1997).

12. Hugh Haughton, 'The White Knight's Cult of Little Girls', *Times Literary Supplement*, August 8 1997, p. 23.

13. Mary Douglas, 'Jokes', in *Implicit Meanings: Essays in Anthropology* (London, 1975), p. 106.

privileges of open speech that are forbidden to others, and can therefore cleanse the community. '[The joker] has a firm hold on his own position in the structure and the disruptive comments he makes upon it are in a sense the comments of the social group upon itself... he lightens for everyone the oppressiveness of social reality, demonstrates its arbitrariness by making light of formality in generality, and expresses the creative possibilities of the situation... his jokes expose the inadequacy of realist structurings of experience and so release the pent-up power of the imagination.'[14]

Lewis Carroll, securely placed in two of the most established high institutions of English life, a fellow of Christ Church College, Oxford, and an ordained deacon in the Church of England, fulfils this paradoxical criterion for the eruption of fooling. It is because the Reverend Charles Dodgson existed that he could also be Lewis Carroll: the two personae, so remarkably inconsistent, meet through the character of joking itself – that it plumbs deep into shared meanings, and those meanings depend on the institutions the joker knows well and can therefore mock percipiently. 'This fellow is wise enough to play the fool,' says Viola of Feste in *Twelfth Night*, 'And to do that well craves a kind of wit... /...This is a practice/ As full of labor as a wise man's art...'[15]

In Lewis Carroll's case, however, he could not have communicated for over a century across languages and cultures from Iceland to Japan if he had only fooled with Victorian values, with the customs of High Table or the Senior Common Room or the doctrinal disputes between Anglicans and Evangelicals. He is slyly funny about these, and also covertly critical of Darwinism, and other 'progressive' ideas of his time, as William Empson observed in his

14. Douglas, 'Jokes', p. 107.

15. William Shakespeare, *Twelfth Night*, Act III, scene 1.

acute essay, '*Alice in Wonderland*: The Child as Swain' (1935).[16] But Carroll also transmuted the material close at hand in his own experiences into blithely comic scenes with pan-cultural appeal. And he was able to do this because he was also deeply rooted in another, far more fundamental but abstract structure: mathematics and formal logic. By playing continually with the rules of language itself, by constantly drawing attention to their breakdown, Lewis Carroll's fantasies become metaphysical fooling with the very ground of meaning itself: exhilarating, unburdening nonsense.

As Hugh Haughton comments in his perceptive introduction to *The Chatto Book of Nonsense Poetry*, the English love of infantile mimicry in the nineteenth century 'forms part of a culture with a huge investment in ideas of social and intellectual authority and a dedication to the idea of moral earnestness – a critique played out in the children's books of Lear and Carroll...'[17] Nonsense rhymes and songs and catches and refrains figure in the literature of many cultures, but they make a particularly strong showing in both oral and written English literature. Noel Malcolm, in *The Origins of English Nonsense*, actually names Sir John Hoskyns (d. 1638) and the 'Water Poet' John Taylor (d. 1653) as the *fons et origo* of the genre as literature; they were Royalists, writing during the Puritan hegemony, and gobbledegook and gibberish – jabberwocky – both provided a shelter for insurrectionary assaults on the Roundheads, and expressed the royalist commitment to the ludic.[18] 'For Nonsense is Rebellion.' wrote Taylor.[19] Though this precise dating may be arguable, the point about the political context is important and too easily overlooked: English power and wealth, intellectual and social self-confidence, as well as the start of far-reaching colonial influence, created a breeding ground for the kind of destabilizing and creative

16. William Empson, '*Alice in Wonderland*: The Child as Swain', in *Some Versions of Pastoral*, (London, 1950), pp. 253-94, 254-6.

17. Hugh Haughton, ed. *The Chatto Book of Nonsense Poetry* (London, 1988), p. 6.

18. Nick Groom, 'A Monstrous Surfeit of Mincing and Galumphing Nuncheons', *Times Higher Education Supplement*, 11 July 1997, p. 22.

19. Noel Malcolm, *The Origins of English Nonsense* (London, 1997), p. 184.

explosions that constitute fantastic nonsense – Jonathan Swift, Henry Fielding, Laurence Sterne, even occasionally Dr. Johnson himself, William Blake, Christopher Smart, all nourish the tradition from which Carroll sprang. The genre of the *Alice* books sidles to the attack through spoofs, pastiche, riddles, and various puckish logophilic word games. It is probably not incidental that Alice Liddell's father was the great Greek lexicographer and that she was brought up in a house of words.[20]

In *Looking-Glass*, the Red Queen remarks in typically cross fashion, 'What do you suppose is the use of a child without any meaning? Even a joke should have some meaning and a child's more important than a joke, I hope.'[21] Carroll thought highly of jokes, and they structured all his exchanges with children; he kept stores of toys and games and puzzles in his rooms and brought them out to play with his visitors, he demonstrated the magic of numbers in mathematics, such as 'mystic nines';[22] he could conjure and do card tricks, knew how to make a paper pistol pop, could make various animals with a folded handkerchief, pass a halfpenny through a sixpenny hole, he invented word games and picture riddles and ways of doing sums which most children found droll and absorbing (though some were bored). And he parodied in life – as in the *Alice* books – solemn lessons and high sentiments and lyric poetry. His nonsense upskittled rules and regulations. The Red Queen wanted things to have meaning, and preferred those meanings to obey rules, however Humpty Dumptyish in their capriciousness. But Carroll does not much like the Red Queen, and he very much liked nonsense.

The figure of the child united the two target arenas of Carroll's

20. Jean-Jacques Lecercle, *The Philosophy of Nonsense: The Intuitions of Victorian Nonsense Literature* (London, 1994), p. 198.

21. Lewis Carroll, *Through the Looking-Glass and What Alice Found There* [Miniature edition 1907] (London, 1940), p. 189.

22. The property of the number nine, whose multiples always add up to nine.

expertise: Victorian polite society and the peculiar illogicalities of common parlance and mores. A child has not yet learned the manners, rules and prejudices that govern the adult world, and sees through them – or rather Carroll could make Alice the vehicle of his own rationality, of his amused detachment from the covenances, and, at other times, his distaste and indignation. His wit attacks hypocrisy: he parodies the gentlemanly codes that govern fighting, most famously in the mock heroic ballad 'Tweedledum and Tweedledee/Agreed to have a battle…', but elsewhere as well. As she watches the duel of the White and Red Knights in *Looking-Glass*, Alice is thinking: 'I wonder what the Rules of Battle are?' She tries to make sense of them, but of course cannot. In *Looking-Glass,* Alice's encounter with Humpty Dumpty is one of the most brilliant (and bruising) skirmishes between the sound good sense (of reasonable, unspoiled minds) that passes for childish nonsense and the irrational (spoiled adult) regimen that passes for sense.[23] Nonsense is 'a mistake on purpose', Susan Stewart writes;[24] Alice's challenge to Humpty Dumpty's distortion of this in the interests of Mastery has become rightly proverbial:

'But "glory" doesn't mean "a nice knock-down argument",'
Alice objected.
'When *I* use a word,' Humpty Dumpty said in rather a scornful tone,
'it means just what I choose it to mean – neither more nor less.'[25]

The Red Queen, as she rampages across the *Looking-Glass* chessboard, personifies even more furiously the arbitrary tyranny of custom and the petty victories scored through the code of etiquette:

'Speak when you're spoken to!' the Queen sharply interrupted her.

23. Lecercle, *Philosophy of Nonsense*, p. 163.

24. Susan Stewart, *Nonsense: Aspects of Intertextuality in Folklore and Literature* (Baltimore, 1989), pp. 49-50, 206.

25. Carroll, *Looking-Glass*, p. 125.

'But if everybody obeyed that rule!' said Alice, who was always ready for a little argument, 'and if you only spoke when you were spoken to, and the other person always waited for *you* to begin, you see nobody would ever say anything, so that –'
'Ridiculous!' cried the Queen.[26]

Another reason for the huge popularity of both *Wonderland* and *Looking-Glass* lies in Carroll's championing of the child against the adult world and its authority; he lampoons adult moralizing through the horrid Duchess in *Alice in Wonderland*, who says, 'Tut, tut, child'.... Every thing's got a moral, if only you can find it.'[27] Unlikely as it may seem, this crabby Oxford don is a natural father to the Woodstock generation. Nevertheless, it is probably a mistake to cast him as a patron saint of hedonist subversion, for his Alice plays one set of rules against another, to show up the inherently comic contradictions that govern day-to-day life.[28]

A girl-child specially embodied the spirit of argument because Carroll knew, from his close acquaintance with so many, that Victorian social pressures and expectations tightlaced growing women into shapes that squeezed out the bright spirit of their childhood. A Victorian woman was expected to put away childish things more definitely than her brother, and had travelled far farther from the character of her youth when she grew up. Alice, his heroine, is outspoken, frank, impatient, quick-witted, adventurous, passionate in her responses, curious, petulant, frequently impertinent and cross. Empson says she is 'rather a pert child... the underdog speaking up for itself...'[29] Alice is 'fresh' in both senses of the term, exhibiting qualities that moralists, from Aristotle and Plutarch onwards, had singled out for condemnation in

26. *Looking-Glass*, p. 187.

27. *Wonderland*, p. 135.

28. Empson, *Some Versions*, p. 279.

29. Empson, *Some Versions*, p. 260.

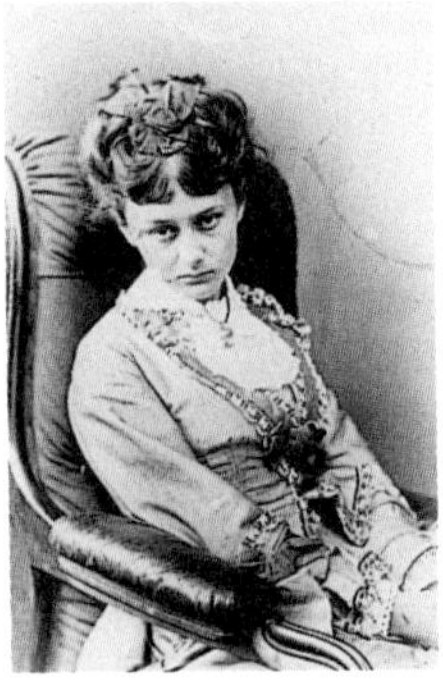

[Figure 2]
Charles Lutwidge Dodgson's
last photograph of
Alice Liddell
taken on June 25 1870

the female sex. She personifies the very antithesis of the subordinate, modest, mute and maidenly angel in the house. If Alice Liddell, on that blissful boat trip that afternoon in 1862, did indeed possess such quantities of sparky effrontery, inquisitiveness and scepticism, then Mrs. Reginald Hargreaves, the married woman Alice became, no longer did; Carroll later wrote her distant letters, and his last photograph of her in 1870, when she was eighteen, shows her sunken into the chair, her arms squeezed by her sides as if, out of frame, she is twisting her hands, her eyes resentful, a whipped bitch kind of a look, not even the faintest ghost of the pert, coquettish little mischief-making madam of her enchanting child-self. It is a sad portrait, but, like so much of Lewis Carroll's photography, it achieves an unsettling collusion with the sitter: the real-life Alice herself a perfect witness to the successful crushing of female personality by Victorian conventional aspirations.

It is striking that when Carroll throws his voice to speak for his ideal audience – to see things as Alice does – his diction and vocabulary and rhythm change. He chooses a comic register, and it entails lots of oos and uus and js and ks and bs (as in 'Jabberwock' and 'Jubjub bird' and 'Bandersnatch' and 'Boojum'). These are hard, percussive sounds found more in Anglo-Saxon attitudes than Victorian sonorities of style, and Carroll's choice assumes that the natural language of a child corresponds to an earlier stratum in the English language itself, before Gallicisms and Latinisms and Hellenisms elongated the vowels and softened and aspirated the consonants and puffed long words and stretched jaunty, bouncy prosodic forms into breathy hexameters. The longing to escape from under the burden of learning into an unintelligible and pristine (uncreated till that moment) babble that communicates directly to the senses, without cultural freighting, marks some of Carroll's greatest work, like 'Jabberwocky' ('A Stanza of Anglo-Saxon Poetry... This curious fragment')[30] as well as the dotty but melancholy delights of *The Hunting of the Snark.*

30. Carroll, *Rectory Umbrella*, p. 139.

Carroll's love of girl children is central to his strangeness, and his interest in expanding the circle of his 'child-friends' unusually assiduous among men of his class and occupation, not only because they were, almost invariably, little girls rather than little boys, but because his appetite for them was oceanic: in 1863 alone, he made a list of 107 he planned to photograph. He was a most dedicated wooer, indefatigable in his enshrinement of their images. Mrs. Liddell, the fussocking mother of Alice, was alerted to something she found untoward, and around the time of Alice's eleventh birthday, there was a rupture. But on the whole, the extent of parental co-operation with Carroll's elaborate plans for treats and outings is remarkable; such entrustment of little girls to a young single male is not usual today.

Part of the fun was Carroll's effervescent parody of grown-up norms: he mimicked for his child visitors all the rituals of seduction. Intimate *tête-à-tête* meals, picnics *al fresco*, rowing on the river, flurried exchanges of *billets-doux*, full of delightful banter and jokes and compliments and fuss and names interlaced in acrostics. He took flattering, lively photographs of his friends for keepsakes, and even, as has become notorious, began asking for his 'child-friends' to pose '*sans habillement*' as he put it – the slide into French surely betraying *pudeur* – in the 1870s, after several years of taking many clothed portraits. One of the nude sessions happened very quickly, very mischievously, when the children ducked under the table cloth and emerged in the buff, on all fours, laughing. Later, he scrupulously negotiated agreement from them and from their parents beforehand. Kisses were his reward for all the forms his attentions took, images, jests, mock lessons: he teases in letters about the giving of kisses, and the taking of them.

The sustained parody of adult wooing in his entertainments was part and parcel of that delighting delinquency that buoys the humour of both *Alice in Wonderland* and *Through the Looking-Glass* as well as the extended poetic fantasy, *The Hunting of the Snark.* His own innocence, of course, depends on the expression of sexuality and the form it took, but his obsession with little girls was expressed in a different context of social and sexual customs; his paedophilia belonged with cultural behaviour and attitudes that made it different from child abuse today.[31] The passionate letters, vows, embraces, tears exchanged between Bettina von Arnim and Karoline von Günderode at the beginning of the nineteenth century do not proclaim the two women were lovers, even though they are expressing and no doubt experiencing fervent pleasure in their love, their contact, their intimacy.[32] But Carroll was aware of problems about his passion: and not just from Mrs. Liddell. He knew perfectly well he could not circulate his photographs of naked children, for example, and he cancelled the plates so that they could not be copied. His behaviour was quite open-eyed, and the avoidance of furtiveness a declaration of independence.

'What are little girls made of?' asks the kind of nursery rhyme Carroll liked to echo. 'Sugar and spice and all that's nice/That's

31. See Carol Mavor, Pleasures Taken: *Performances of Sexuality and Loss in Victorian Photographs* (Durham, 1995), pp. 7-42 for an extended and sensitively-argued analysis of Carroll's photographs of children.

32. Bettina von Arnim, 'Report on Günderode's Suicide', in *Bitter Healing: German Women Writers 1700-1830*, eds. Jeannine Blackwell and Susanne Zantop (Lincoln, 1990), pp. 455-72.

what little girls are made of.' In this piece of proverbial wisdom, little boys, by contrast, are made of 'frogs and snails and puppy-dogs' tails'. (The Opies comment that the rhyme has been attributed to Robert Southey, but that they cannot find it in his works.)[33] Lewis Carroll liked giving his little girlfriends tea, but unlike the Mad Hatter, he always provided jam, as he carefully explained to one mother as he issued the invitation. He himself ate very little: one meal a day, only. He was ram-rod straight to the end of his life, thin as a rail, and thought little of taking twenty-five mile walks. But he understood the pleasures of sitting down together to eat – and indeed, when he volunteered his services as Curator of Christ Church's common room, he took charge of the college's catering and introduced the custom of afternoon tea there for the first time.

For a man who was so austere in his tastes, food held his interest and dominates the imagery of his jokes from his juvenilia onwards. Indeed he sounded a nostalgic note for such childhood pleasures as early as 1854, when he was already recalling lost times of pinafores, treacle and innocence'.[34] This closeness to children's primal appetites he retained all his life: puddings and pies, tarts, cakes, and treacle wells recur alongside more elaborate fare, oysters and lobsters and mock turtle soup.

'I know *something* interesting is sure to happen,' she [Alice] said to herself, 'whenever I eat or drink anything; so I'll just see what this little bottle does.'[35] (Not a scene that would be allowed in today's children's writing.) Carroll is at his most effervescently inventive when his fantasies are trained on eating and drinking: in one early story, the villain – an early Boojum – gets reduced to 'mashed potatoe' (sic).[36] Alice finds an – empty – pot of marmalade down

33. Iona and Peter Opie, eds., *The Oxford Dictionary of Nursery Rhymes* (Oxford, 1977), pp. 100-1.

34. Carroll, 'Wilhelm Von Schmitz' in *The Whitby Gazette*, 1854. I am most grateful to Michael Bakewell for this reference.

35. Carroll, *Wonderland*, p. 46.

36. Carroll, *Rectory Umbrella*, pp. 76-7.

the rabbit-hole, and in a letter to Mary MacDonald Carroll recommended a remedy for her kitten's tooth-ache: 'wash it carefully in hasty-puding, and give it 4 pin-cushions boiled in sealing-wax, and just dip the end of its tail in hot coffee.'[37] The proprieties of food offered the absurdist in Carroll another system to juggle with, and with the Mock Turtle's instructions to the Lobster Quadrille, he grasped 'the innate hilarity of animated food', of gourmandizing and surfeit which enlivens many an earlier nonsense poem.[38] Again, he makes inspired mischief with expected categories of right things to eat and wrong things to eat, until one can almost hear children's protesting laughter bubbling up from the page. Among his other inventions, the White Knight passes on a recipe for pudding:

'It began with blotting-paper,'...
'That wouldn't be very nice, I'm afraid –'
'Not very nice alone,' he interrupted, quite eagerly:
'but you've no idea what a difference it makes,
mixing it with other things –
such as gunpowder and sealing-wax.'[39]

At other times, Carroll displays his humour in its most dangerous and even perverse mood, as in the 'Pig & Pepper' episode, which he added to the original manuscript of *Wonderland.* He stages a ferocious culinary assault on a baby: the Nurse seems to be dressing it for the Duchess to dine on, and it then turns into a piglet in Alice's arms: 'And she began thinking over other children she knew, who might do very well as pigs...'.[40] (Harry Graham may be echoing the scene with one of his *Ruthless Rhymes for Heartless Homes*:

37. Carroll, *Looking-Glass Letters*, p. 63.

38. Groom, *'Monstrous Surfeit'*, p. 22.

39. Carroll, *Looking-Glass*, p. 176.

40. Carroll, *Wonderland*, p. 91.

41. Carroll, *Looking-Glass*, p. 77.

Nurse, [who] peppered baby's face
(She mistook it for a muffin)...
Mother, seeing baby blinded,
Said, 'Oh, nurse, how absent-minded.')

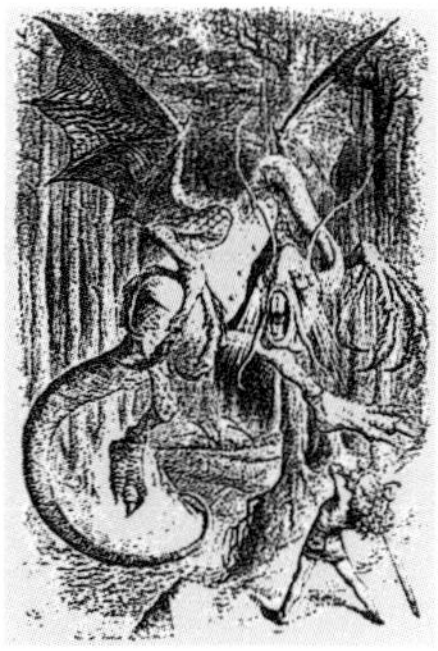

[Figure 3]
Sir John Tenniel's illustration of the Jabberwock

Then, in *Looking-Glass*, the fantasies about who gets eaten take a turn into gallows humour:

'Now if you're ready, Oysters dear,
We can begin to feed.'

'But not on us!' the Oysters cried,
Turning a little blue.[41]

But the Oysters are 'eaten every one', as the Walrus and the Carpenter weep crocodile tears. Tenniel's illustration of the Jabberwock, Carroll's nursery bogey to end all bogeys ('The jaws that bite, the claws that catch!') was considered too successful in its horror to be used as the frontispiece, as originally planned.

Towards the end of his life, in 1889, Carroll wrote from Hatfield House to the child actress Isa Bowman, one of the last and closest of his child-friends. He told her that he had recently met Princess Alice, the daughter of Queen Victoria's son, Prince Leopold, who was probably named after Alice Liddell and Carroll's heroine. Carroll jokes to Isa: 'Now that I have made friends with a real live little Princess, I don't intend ever to *speak* to any more children that haven't titles. In fact I'm so proud and I hold my chin so high [doodled portrait of himself thus supplied] that I shouldn't even *see* you if we met!' But then he rushes on without a break to reassure her: 'No darling, you mustn't believe *that.* If I made friends with a *dozen* Princesses I would love you better than all of them together, even [if] I had them all rolled up into a sort of child-roly-poly.'[42] So the teatime treats return to convey just how sweet and spicy is the stuff little girls are made of. If kissing can be 'aim-inhibited eating', as Adam Phillips has suggested in his essay, 'Plotting for Kisses',[43] then Carroll's fascination with tea parties, and jam tarts, and his recurrent fantasies about the jaws that bite, about babies that turn into pigs and get their faces peppered, with old men devouring little oysters, become moves in his unconscious – and in his plot.

42. Cohen, *Lewis Carroll*, p. 477.

43. Adam Phillips, *On Kissing, Tickling and Being Bored: Psychoanalytic Essays on the Unexamined Life* (London, 1993), p. 103.

44. Carroll, *Looking-Glass*, pp. 150-1.

In *Through the Looking-Glass* the author meditates more deeply on the nature of a child than he had done in *Wonderland.* Haigha the Messenger explains Alice to the Unicorn: ' "This is a child!... We only found it to-day. It's as large as life, and twice as natural!" ' At this, the Unicorn exclaims, ' "I always thought they were fabulous monsters!... Is it alive?" "It can talk," said Haigha, solemnly.' Alice retorts that she thought that 'Unicorns were fabulous monsters, too'. The two of them strike a 'bargain' and agree to believe in each other.[44]

It would provoke a little girl to be called a fabulous monster and referred to as an 'it'; it would entertain future child listeners and readers to be whisked out of reality into the domain of unicorns and other wonders – or, to put it looking-glass fashion, to have such wonders conjured as real. But to be 'large as life and twice as natural' is perhaps a more revealing casual exclamation: the naturalness of pre-gendered young girls embodied for Lewis Carroll the Romantic ideal, announced by Blake and Wordsworth and Coleridge, free spirits possessing untrammelled innocence, in a providential state of natural virtue. He took a photograph of Alice Liddell in rags, cupping her hand to play 'a beggar maid'[45]: little girls, begging for gifts of any kind, questioning little girls in bare feet, became for him the flesh and blood equivalent of this state of language, this state of the soul, this state of the imagination.

45. See plate on page 66.

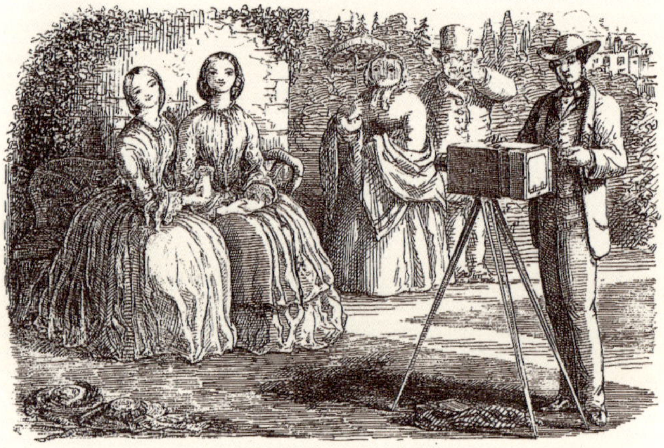

ONE OF THE PLEASURES OF PHOTOGRAPHY.— VISITING COUNTRY HOUSES AND CALOTYPING ALL THE ELIGIBLE DAUGHTERS.

BY ROGER TAYLOR

Although Charles Dodgson's reputation today rests largely upon his published writings under the pseudonym of Lewis Carroll, his contribution to the history of photography was equally remarkable. When he took up photography as an amateur in 1856, Dodgson was a young man. Over the next twenty-four years he pursued this 'other occupation' with a vigour and passion which sets him apart from his contemporaries.[1] [Figure 5]

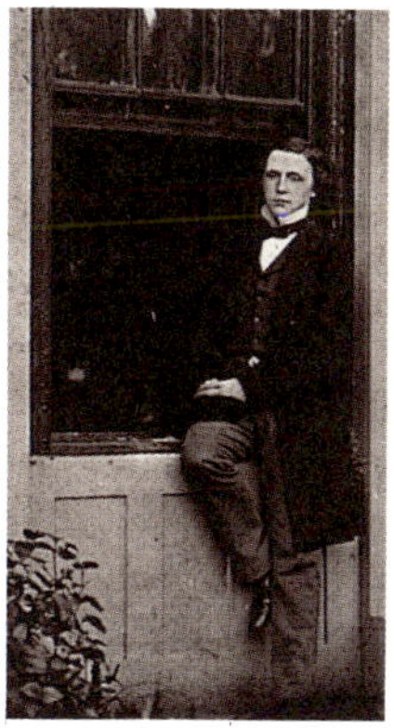

[Figure 5]
Portrait of Charles Dodgson as a young man. Ref # p. 237
NPG, London

[Figure 4] *Opposite*
'One of the pleasures of Photography – Visiting Country Houses and Calotyping all the Eligible Daughters', *Photographic Pleasures...*
Private Collection

1. The title and quotation is taken from a letter Dodgson wrote to his Uncle Skeffington Lutwidge asking him 'to get me a photographic apparatus, as I want some other occupation here than mere reading and writing.' Quoted by Morten N. Cohen, *Lewis Carroll, A Biography*, London, 1995, p.60.

Photography first came before the public in 1839. During the first decade of development it was widely regarded as either a scientific curiosity used by a few wealthy individuals for their personal pleasure, or as the vehicle of tradesmen who took commercial photographic portraits. Like all new inventions of significance, photography's first decade was a period of rapid improvement and advance, with each new chemical formula and design improvement stepping on the shoulders of its predecessor. In the nation that was at the very forefront of industrialization, manufacture and commercialism, it is not surprising that both of the principal photographic processes, one French, the other British, were surrounded from the outset with restrictive patents. Effectively, these patents did more to inhibit the expansion of photography than perhaps any other factor. As late as 1850, only a select few of Britain's population had seen a photograph, let alone understood its conceptual framework.

Despite these constraints, photography gradually found its strength, composure and self-assurance and during the 1850s, the initial promise held out by photography during the previous decade, was progressively realized as one event followed another to shape the public attitude.

The Great Exhibition of 1851, held in Hyde Park, was the first public exhibition at which photographs were shown. At one level it allowed commercial portrait photographers to present their best work and camera manufacturers to reveal their latest technological advances. It also presented the medium for the first time as a means of artistic self-expression.[2] Writing about his own visit to the Crystal Palace, Dodgson does not mention seeing the photographs. But given his love of gadgets and mechanical devices, he would probably have been more attracted to the instruments, where telescopes, barometers, microscopes and scientific instruments were exhibited alongside daguerreotype portraits and the cameras that made them.

With so much diversity and spectacle on view at the Great Exhibition, the display of photography was rather overshadowed. As a result, a small group of photographers proposed the idea of mounting a large-scale photographic exhibition at the Society of Arts in London. The exhibition opened in December 1852 with nearly 800 photographs on display. This was the first independent exhibition of its kind and marks the full-scale emergence of photography into the public domain.

Encouraged by the success of their exhibition, the same group of photographers established a Photographic Society in London whose guiding principle was to be 'the promotion of the Art and Science of Photography, by the interchange of thought and experience.'[3] Membership was drawn largely from the professional classes where income and leisure allowed photography to be taken up more readily. For the most part, members of the Photographic Society were individuals who practised the medium for personal development and not immediate profit. Even though this was an

2. British photographs could be seen at the Great Exhibition within the displays of *Philosophical, Musical, Horological and Surgical Instruments, Class X*, and in *Fine Arts, Class XXX*. The extensive displays submitted by foreign countries also included photographs. Pre-eminent among these were France and America. One estimate suggests that over 700 photographs were on display. For a more detailed listing of exhibits see the *Official Descriptive and Illustrated Catalogue*, London, 3 vols., 1851.

3. The Photographic Society of London was formally established at a meeting held at the Society of Arts, London, on 20th January 1853, at which the aims and governing principles were agreed by all present. A report of the meeting is given in *The Journal of the Photographic Society*, 3 March 1853, vol. 1, n. 1, p. 1. from which this quote is taken.

ethos with which Dodgson could readily identify, he never chose to join this, or any other Photographic Society.[4]

Several other factors were also at work during the first half of the decade. In keeping with the spirit of optimism that followed in the wake of the Great Exhibition, the British inventor of photography, Henry Fox Talbot, was prevailed upon to relinquish his photographic patent. By this single, generous act, photography was liberated from the cobweb of restrictions which had held it down for more than a decade.[5] Once released, photography burgeoned at an unprecedented rate. Instrument makers designed and manufactured splendid mahogany and brass cameras, opticians offered newly-improved lenses; chemists brought out enhanced formulae for photographic solutions; handbooks on manipulation were published that promised to reveal the secrets of photographic success.[6] Exhibitions were sent on tour around the nation, even to remote market towns and villages. Here, landscape and architectural studies by some of Britain's leading photographers were seen by a larger segment of society than ever before.[7] In the wake of these exhibitions and in response to the ready availability of apparatus and chemistry, photographic societies began to spring up around Britain.[8] Such unprecedented activity made photography an increasingly fashionable pastime within polite society. It was so widely accepted it became the subject of satire.

The Reverend Edward Bradley, under the pseudonym of Cuthbert Bede, published *Photographic Pleasures Popularly Portrayed with Pen and Pencil*, in March 1855.[9] The alliterative title reveals much about Bradley's approach to the subject. Throughout the text he uses puns to play upon the meanings of newly-coined photographic terms.

4. Even though he was related to Sir Frederick Pollock, President of the Photographic Society of London, Dodgson never became a member and only once submitted work to the Annual Exhibition. [See note 25] His uncle Skeffington Lutwidge was, however, an active member, contributing prints to exhibitions and the Exchange Club Albums that circulated among members. See Seiberling & Bloor, *Amateurs, Photography, and the Mid-Victorian Imagination*, Chicago & London, 1986

5. The bitter controversy surrounding Talbot's photographic patent and the manner in which it is supposed to have limited the growth of photography prior to 1852 is a complex matter that has yet to be thoroughly researched. The most comprehensive account can be found in Larry J. Schaaf, *Out of the Shadows: Herschel, Talbot & the Invention of Photography*, London, 1992, pp. 158-161

6. The literature of photography is rich with handbooks and manuals detailing the methods of working individual processes. Retailers with a commercial interest in photography issued any number of guides, frequently issued in several editions as improvement followed improvement. Twenty-one handbooks, catalogues, manuals and instruction leaflets are listed by Helmut Gernsheim, *Incunabula of British Photographic Literature* 1839-1875, London, 1984, pp. 100-103

7. In 1853, following the success of its Photographic Exhibition, the Society of Arts took the initiative to create a further exhibition drawing upon work by the best photographers. This was sent on tour to eighteen cities and towns throughout Britain in 1853 and 1854. It proved so successful that two further exhibitions were shown in thirty-four centres throughout 1854 and 1855. For outline details see *Journal of the Society of Arts*, 4 March 1853, NS v1, p. 175

Negatives and positives, developing solutions and getting in a fix, was the currency of his language. Bradley's wonderful illustrations capture something of the thrill and excitement that surrounded photography. Significantly, he suggested photography was such a novelty that young men in possession of a camera would have the means of entry into fashionable society. Eligible young ladies would readily agree to 'sit' before the camera. Children would stand captivated at the antics of the photographer beneath his black focussing cloth. Later, when the results were printed, albums of photographs would become the objects of admiration at tea parties. Photography, it was suggested, was a social and artistic adventure for a young man wishing to advance himself in the eyes of others. [Figure 4 page 26.]

To Dodgson, photography must have seemed a heaven-sent pastime. Taking Bradley at his word, it could be the means of access into the richer layers of Oxford society where, for a young man embarking on an academic career, such contacts and friendships were essential to advancement. But the appeal of photography to Dodgson lay not just in its social acceptability. To his fertile and receptive mind it offered the perfect balance between science and art, chemistry and aesthetics, gadgetry and practicality. At heart, Dodgson longed to be an artist and wished he were more competent at sketching and drawing. For nearly twenty-five years photography became the agency by which he made pictures, a means of self-expression that was to become his consuming pastime.

Initially, there was just one drawback, the cost. During the first years of the 1850s Dodgson was not in a position to afford this expensive diversion. Even though his undergraduate life at Oxford had been

8. For a detailed study of this phenomena see the article by Jens Jaeger, 'Photographic Societies in Britain in the 19th century,' *Darkness and Light*, Proceedings of the ESHP Symposium, Oslo, 1994. pp. 133-140. Jaeger lists over thirty societies that were established during the period 1852-1861.

9. Cuthbert Bede, [pseud. Edward Bradley] *Photographic Pleasures Popularly Portrayed with Pen and Pencil*, London, 1855.

marked by brilliant achievement in mathematics, his academic future remained uncertain. Even after his appointment as a Tutor at the College in the spring of 1855, his financial prospects were precarious. Unlike many young men at Oxford he could not fall back on the financial support of his family.[10]

It was only towards the end of 1855 that his ambition to become a Mathematical Lecturer was realized. With the appointment came a salary of £300 per annum, more than sufficient for a young man of twenty-four to have financial independence. Dodgson recognized his good fortune, noting in his diary :

> 'I am sitting alone in my bedroom this last night of the old year, waiting for midnight. It has been the most eventful year of my life: I began it a poor bachelor student with no definite plans or expectations; I end it a master and tutor in Christ Church, with an income of more than £300 a year, and the course of mathematical tuition marked out by God's providence for at least some years to come. Great Mercies, great failings, time lost, talents misapplied – such has been the past year.'[11]

This improvement in his fortunes allowed him to buy a photographic outfit, complete with the latest design of camera, lenses, tripod, chemicals, dippers, droppers, tongs and trays.[12] The whole ensemble would have cost him at least £25, a considerable sum to invest, but one that Dodgson no doubt thought worthwhile for the promise it held of establishing new contacts within the academic community, as well as being an outlet for his artistic expression.[13]

10. The Dodgson family, though socially well connected, never had the financial independence associated with the landed aristocracy and gentry whose sons were such a feature of undergraduate life at the University. Whilst at Daresbury Dodgson's father enjoyed the modest income of a Curate. Only with the move to Croft did the fortunes of the family improve. But with a large family to support and appearances to maintain, frugality and prudence became a way of life.

11. Quoted in Stuart Dodgson Collingwood, *The Life and Letters of Lewis Carroll*, London, 1898, pp. 64-65.

12. The camera Dodgson bought had been designed and handcrafted by Ottewill at his 'manufactory' in Islington, North London. It was also available from the eminent optician Andrew Ross. The camera was advertised as being 'superior to every other form of Camera, from its capability of elongation or contraction to any focal adjustment, its portability and adaptation for taking either views or portraits.' The advanced design allowed the body of the camera to collapse from a cube into a flat pack. See *Journal of the Photographic Society*, v.1, n.12, p. 141, for Ottewill's advertisement. Dodgson notes in his diary the cost of his camera was 'about £15'.

13. The cost of setting oneself up in photography was considerable. A contemporary manufacturer's catalogue reveals that with all the essential bits and pieces Dodgson would have had very little change from £25. See *Horne, Thornthwaite, and Wood's, Catalogue of Photographic Apparatus and Chemical Preparations*, London, nd. 1852, reprinted Bloomfield Books, 1974.

At another level, the practice of photography would have appealed to his love of order and discipline. He was an obsessive maker of lists, using them to exercise control over his social and professional life. By the end of his life he indexed nearly 100,000 letters of both incoming and outgoing mail.[14] The complex nature of mid-nineteenth-century photography demanded careful control. There were exposures to be noted and equations for the optical and chemical focus to be resolved with each exposure. The wet collodion process he used throughout his photographic career was ticklishly difficult to work. Success came only with the complete mastery of its complex chemistry. Nothing could be left to chance; otherwise the negative was spoiled. There were delicate varnishes to be applied, negatives and prints to be numbered and registered, albums of finished work to be sequenced and mounted, and lists of sitters to be compiled.[15 16]

Even the conceptual framework of photography would have appealed to Dodgson's fertile and surreal imagination. Through the ground glass of his camera his view of the world have been turned upside down and laterally inverted. The foreground took the place of sky; what lay to the right now appeared on the left; people hung upside down, large things were reduced in scale. Adjust the camera and small things were enlarged. Twiddle the focus of the lens and the outlines of solid objects dissolved until they disappeared from view. In the deep red light of the dark room there was other magic at work. The alchemy of developing solutions made images appear out of thin air; the invisible becoming visible, the third dimension reduced to two. Watching the glass plate develop offered a conundrum of reversed tones where white became black and black, white. The positive had become negative; the negative, positive.

14. Donald Rakin deals with this obsessive aspect of Dodgson's personality at length in his essay 'Blessed Rage: Lewis Carroll and the Modern Quest for Order.' See Edward Guiliano, ed. *Lewis Carroll: A Celebration,* New York, 1992, pp. 15-25.

15. Dodgson numbered both his negatives and prints in separate running sequences. The negative sequence is impossible to follow as Dodgson recycled his glass plates, reassigning old negative numbers as he went along. The print numbers are both logical and chronological in their order and it is these which have been cited in this catalogue. Dodgson compiled at least ten main Photograph Albums. Each has a carefully prepared index of subjects and sitters, cross-referenced to the print number. He also made up albums for presentation to friends. A number of these albums, along with other important material, are at the Firestone Library, University of Princeton, and the Gernsheim Collection, Harry Ransom Humanities Research Center, University of Texas, Austin, The National Portrait Gallery, London and Christ Church Library, Oxford.

16. Dodgson's diary for March 1863 lists 108 names 'photographed or to be photographed.' Ibid., Cohen, *Lewis Carroll, A Biography*, London, 1995, p. 160.

In the world of photography the transient became permanent and the established, fugitive. Nothing was ever quite what it seemed. To the imagination of the man who was to write *Alice's Adventures in Wonderland* and *Through the Looking-Glass and What Alice Found There*, this must have been infinitely appealing.

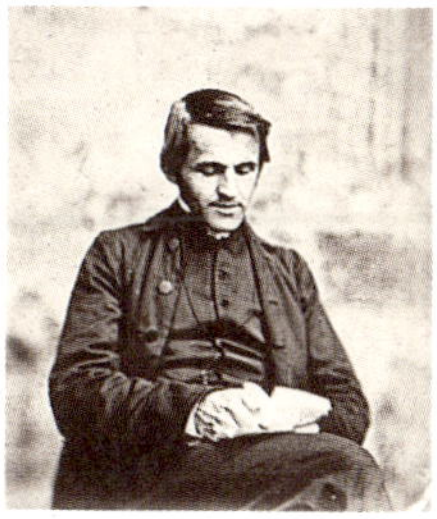

[Figure 6]
Dr. Henry Parry Liddon.
NPG p. 7/22, London

Unlike the vast majority of amateur photographers of this period, Dodgson was little interested in taking landscape views or topographic studies of crumbling ruins. His primary interest was in portraiture, perhaps the most difficult and certainly the most elusive of photographic subjects, but potentially the most rewarding. Successful portraiture requires rapport between photographer and sitter. Dodgson, always interested in the beauty and nature of his fellow beings, used his camera to explore and define the personality of his sitter through their pose, expression and setting. In this he was supremely self-confident and masterful. Unlike the average studio photographer, where a sitting would have been over in a matter of minutes, one feels that Dodgson was prepared to devote considerable time to each pose, putting his sitters at ease and allowing them to adopt relaxed, natural poses.

This comes across in his extended series of portraits of fellow dons at Oxford. One of the most intimate is of his close friend, Henry Liddon. It was with Liddon that Dodgson made his only trip abroad when they visited Russia in 1867. Liddon suggested the title of *Through the Looking-Glass*. Despite the long exposure, Liddon looks completely relaxed, occupying himself throughout with a bundle of papers on his knee. Even with his downward glance one senses the warmth and strength of his personality. This is a portrait that suggests both sitter and photographer were at ease with each other. [Figure 6]

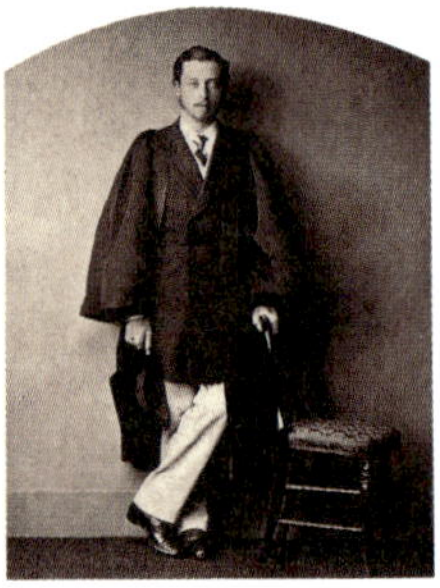

[Figure 7]
Prince Leopold, Christ Church, 2 June 1875, Call # 964:0001 Gernsheim, HRHRC, Texas

When photographing an eminent person Dodgson adopted a different relationship, one that was less assured, allowing the sitter to retain a greater degree of self-control. Perhaps the most distinguished of Dodgson's sitters was Prince Leopold, Queen Victoria's youngest son, newly arrived as an undergraduate at Christ Church. Dodgson photographed him against the plainest of backgrounds and with the simplest of props in the studio he had erected on the roof of Christ Church, above his rooms.[17] As a member of the Royal Family, Leopold was familiar with the whole procedure of photographic portraiture.[18] This familiarity allowed him to be completely at ease with his setting, looking directly into the eye of Dodgson's camera. His self-assured pose leaves no doubt as to his status as a son of the monarch. [Figure 7]

The royal sitting was undoubtedly extremely important to the class conscious Dodgson for the social advantages it would bring.[19] Much rested on the success of his exposures, but neither of the negatives he made met his exacting standards. He noted in his diary 'I took two photographs of him, but neither was quite free from moving.'[20] What a disappointment it must have been.

From the very start, Dodgson understood the value of adding photographs of the rich and famous to his collection. He knew how influential such images were in establishing his position as an artist. His photograph albums were carefully sequenced to reveal the full range of his creative abilities and social contacts within the worlds of art, literature, and the theatre. He travelled everywhere with these albums which became the means of starting conversations, discovering new sitters and striking up friendships, some of which were to last throughout his life. His photographs of Millais, Rossetti,

17. Carroll persuaded the College authorities to allow him to erect a 'glass house' portrait studio on the roof of the College overlooking Tom Quad. The building was completed by October 1871, and once it was fitted out and its heating installed, it was ready for use. Dodgson made his first photograph in the studio on 16 March, 1872.

18. As a member of the Royal Family, Prince Leopold was photographed constantly, either in professional portrait studios or more informally by his elder brother Prince Alfred. For an examples of both see Dimond and Taylor, *Crown and Camera*, London, 1987, p. 161. & p. 201.

19. After seeing a group of child actors at the Haymarket Theatre Dodgson recounted to his brother 'There was not much real beauty [in the little actresses], but 2 or 3 of them would have been much admired, I think, if they had been born in higher stations of life.' This and other examples cited in Cohen, *Lewis Carroll, A Biography*, London, 1995, pp. 300-301.

20. Ibid., Cohen, *Lewis Carroll, A Biography*, London, 1995, p. 161.

Tennyson, Ruskin, Ellen Terry and others acted as his calling cards within society. [Plates pages 52, 53,54]

Unlike his counterparts from commercial portrait studios where large sums of money could be had from publishing photographs of celebrities, Dodgson regarded his photographs as being essentially personal, confined to those within his circle and never intended for public distribution or display. Instead they were gifts 'from the artist' to friends and acquaintances.

But of all Dodgson's photography, it is his portraits of children that singularly mark him out from all his contemporaries. No other photographer was able to capture so perfectly the essence of Victorian childhood, filled as it was by a mixture of vulnerability and play, naiveté and self-awareness. [Plate page 57]

Throughout Dodgson's lifetime the conditions of public health and infant mortality improved only marginally. Especially at risk were the very young , who died in large numbers, many before their first birthdays. Those who did survive, faced death or disability from the childhood diseases of measles, chicken-pox, scarlet fever and whooping cough. Periodically the nation was swept by outbreaks of cholera and typhus that killed young and old, rich and poor alike. Death was ever-present and for those children who remained fit and healthy, the gift of life was seen as a gift from God.[21]

Within this context, it is not surprising that the children in Dodgson's portraits are frequently idealized, sometimes to the point of sentimentality. But we also know that Dodgson revered all aspects of childhood, believing that young children were pure, untouched

21. The topic of public health in Victorian Britain is comprehensively covered by Anthony S. Wohl, *Endangered Lives, Public Health in Victorian Britain*, London, 1983. Under Chapter 2, 'The massacre of the Innocents' infant mortality is dealt with in some detail.

by the sins of the world. He sought them out at every opportunity and never felt more at ease than in their presence.[22] They were his preferred company. Unlike the majority of Victorian parents, he related to children at their own level, never treating them as if they were little grown-ups subject to adult rules and etiquette. Capable of child-like behaviour, he made an endearing friend, entertaining their fertile minds with his fantastical stories, magical tricks and kindness. Whereas in his adult relationships he was all propriety and pedantry, with children he was the very opposite, allowing a degree of informality and behaviour that permitted them to appear before his camera with untidy hair and clothes.[23] What mattered most was a child's natural behaviour. He was quite prepared to set aside normal conventions if it allowed the children to feel more comfortable and lead to a better picture. [Plate page 60]

The cross face of Irene MacDonald defies all Victorian photographic orthodoxy when she poses as having just risen from bed, standing barefoot in a crumpled night dress, hair brush in one hand, a mirror in the other complaining 'It won't come smooth.' The subject matter is not an image of idealized childhood, but reveals what it was like to be a child with unmanageably long hair. [Plate page 63]

Acting out scenes in costume enlivened the daily routine of Victorian family life. It was common to have the children of the household put on some little play or charade for their elders. Queen Victoria and Prince Albert, who encouraged their children to dress up in elaborate costumes and act out charades, made this pastime fashionable.[24] Dodgson happily encouraged his child sitters to dress up and act out roles from their childhood stories. He kept a supply of clothes and theatrical props in his rooms for just this

22. Dodgson's relationship with children has been the subject of much exaggerated and fanciful speculation. What is clear is his necessity for their friendship and companionship throughout his life. For a balanced view of the matter see Cohen *Lewis Carroll, A Biography*, London, 1995, p. 174. He remarks 'He sought them out singly and in groups, while walking in parks and along the beach, on railway journeys, in homes, in theater [sic] dressing rooms, in classrooms.' See Cohen *Lewis Carroll, A Biography*, London, 1995, pp. 104-121.

23. Ibid., Cohen, *Lewis Carroll, A Biography*, London, 1995, p. 162.

24. There are a number of photographs of the Royal children in costume and fancy dress. Examples show the young princes dressed either as Sikh princes or two naked putti in the manner of Raphael's *Sistine Madonna*. See Dimond and Taylor, *Crown and Camera*, pp. 113 & 135.

purpose. The children could be whatever their imagination desired, a Chinaman, a knight in shining armour, St. George slaying the dragon, or 'Little Red Riding Hood' from Grimm's fairy tales.[25] [Plates pages 64, 68, 69]

But of all Dodgson's costume portraits it is that of Alice Liddell as *The Beggar Maid* that is the most memorable. The young girl, subject and inspiration of both *Alice* books, has dressed up as a ragged beggar. She stands barefoot, hand cupped to receive alms, whilst looking steadily into the eye of the camera with a gaze that is both knowing and innocent. A distinguishing feature of beggars everywhere. [Plate page 66]

This photograph of Alice has much in common with the work of another important mid-nineteenth century photographer Oscar Rejlander, a Swedish artist turned photographer specializing in genre studies. His photographs drew high critical praise for the sentiments they expressed when shown in London. They drew equal approval from Dodgson who bought a number of prints in order to study Rejlander's technique, mounting them in a special album entitled *Professional and Other Photographs*.[26] Dodgson's photography is also similar in style and content to the work of other leading photographers of the day, notably Lady Hawarden and Julia Margaret Cameron. But the similarity ends there. Dodgson always managed to retain his own visual identity, never falling into the trap of copying those he admired. Instead, he built upon their example, applying his fertile imagination to each new composition.

Dodgson's photographic career spanned twenty-four years from May 1856 until July 1880, when he finally laid aside his camera.

25. This photograph was one of a group of four that Dodgson submitted in a single frame to the Annual Exhibition of the Photographic Society in 1858. It was hung alongside studies and portraits by some of London's leading commercial photographers. It drew no comment from the critics and Dodgson never exhibited again. An English translation of *Grimm's Fairy Tales* was published in London early 1855 under the title *Grimm's Home Stories,* where they drew adverse criticism for the 'falsehood, disobedience, cunning and cruelty', which lay at their heart. See the brief review in *The Athenaeum*, 3 February 1855, n. 1423, p. 14.

26. Rejlander was one of the leading 'Art' photographers of the mid-nineteenth century. He exhibited widely from 1855 onwards. Dodgson may have first seen his work at the 1856 Exhibition of the Photographic Society of London that he visited in January of that year. Among Rejlander's most popular subjects were children dressed as street beggars, first begun around 1860. The most famous of these was Poor Jo, a ragged, barefoot orphan, hunched in a street doorway, desolate and alone. The only biography is by E. Y. Jones, *Father of Art Photography: O. G. Rejlander* 1813-1875, Newton Abbot, 1973. The album *Professional and Other Photographs* is in the Gernsheim Collection, Harry Ransom Humanities Research Center, The University of Texas at Austin.

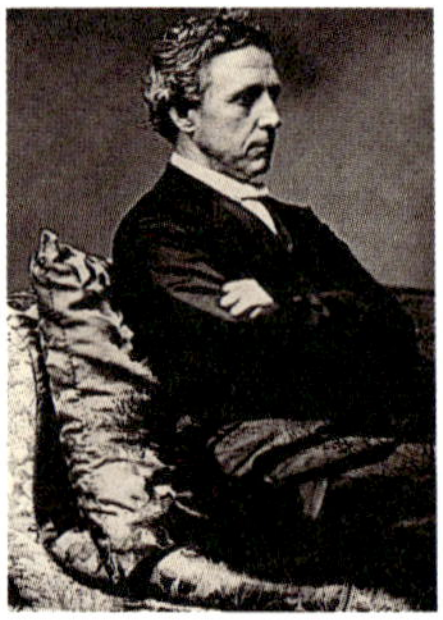

[Figure 8]
Portrait of Charles Dodgson in later life.
Photographer unknown.
Dodgson Family Collection, Surrey History Service

During that time, he pursued his 'other occupation' with great vigour and application. It occupied his routine and filled his diary with endless notes of photographic sessions. Like so much else about Dodgson, his photography borders on the obsessive. Over time it progressed beyond being merely an occupation, to being his means of reaching out and being with others, especially children and more especially female children. To him, photography was as much a means to an end, as an end in itself. [Figure 8]

In this, Dodgson was not unlike many of his fellow academics who, for their 'other occupation' explored the natural world, collecting rocks, butterflies, ferns, fossils and exotic plants, bringing back to their rooms specimens which they carefully labelled, classified and put safely away for future contemplation. Whilst these collectors used nets, traps, bottles and blotting paper to capture and preserve their prey, Dodgson used the seductive lure of his camera and his winning personality to capture young children upon his collodion plates, preserving their knowing innocence forever.

LEWIS CARROLL

BY MICHAEL BAKEWELL

Charles Lutwidge Dodgson, 'Lewis Carroll', was born on 27 January 1832 in the remote country parish of Daresbury in Cheshire, where his father was curate. He was the eldest son in a family of seven sisters and four brothers. As a small boy, according to his nephew, 'he made pets of the most odd and unlikely animals, and numbered certain snails and toads among his intimate friends'. He also developed an early interest in mathematics, which was to be the abiding preoccupation of his life.

By the time the family moved to Croft in Yorkshire on his father's appointment as rector there in 1843, Dodgson had established himself as the children's leader, entertainer and poet laureate:

Sister!, do not raise my wrath,
I'd make you into mutton broth
As easily as kill a moth!

He edited and wrote most of the family magazines and wrote and acted plays for the children's marionette theatre. He invented their games, astounded them with his conjuring tricks, baffled them with conundrums and mazes and ciphers. All his life he would delight in puzzles, whether he was intriguing little children with riddles or infuriating elderly academics with problems in logic. In 1844 he went to school at nearby Richmond where the Headmaster reported that the boy had 'an uncommon share of genius'. Two years later he was sent away to Rugby School; his life there was made miserable by bullying and he later declared that no 'earthly consideration' would induce him to repeat the experience. Nevertheless, he carried off a formidable number of prizes.

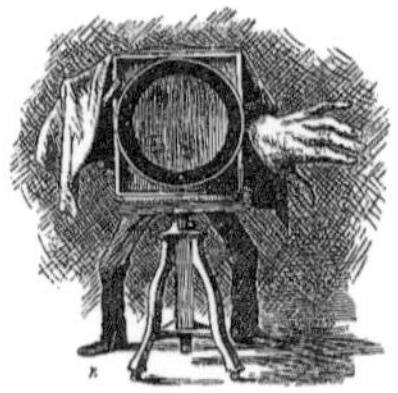

[Figure 9]
Lewis Carroll's 'Hiawatha's Photographing' (1857) details the extreme complication of early photography – 'Mystic, awful was the process.'

On 24 January 1851, Dodgson entered Christ Church College, Oxford. Two days later his mother died, an event of which he never spoke. He so distinguished himself academically that he was made a permanent member of the College the following year, on condition that he remained a bachelor and took Holy Orders. He never married, was ordained in 1861 and was to remain at Christ Church all his life. In 1855 he was made a Lecturer in Mathematics; but he was not a popular tutor and his lectures were described as 'dull as ditchwater'. He himself found 'goading unwilling men to learning they have no taste for' a thankless task. All the same he remained at the post until 1881 and published upwards of thirty books and pamphlets on algebra, geometry and pure mathematics.

From his childhood onwards Dodgson had produced a steady stream of poems and stories full of the particular brand of 'nonsense' he was to make his own. At Oxford he began to contribute verses, parodies and comic pieces to the popular magazines of the day, and it was for these that he devised his pen-name 'Lewis Carroll', a puzzle in itself, consisting of his first names reversed and disguised. In 1856 he was initiated into the 'black art' of photography by his Uncle Skeffington and bought photographic apparatus of his own. It proved a difficult craft to master and he chronicled the miseries of the Victorian photographer in his Longfellow parody *Hiawatha's Photographing* and his story 'A Photographer's Day Out'.

It was while he was trying to take a photograph of Oxford Cathedral that he first made the acquaintance of the little daughters of the Dean of Christ Church, Lorina, Alice and Edith Liddell. They rapidly became 'excellent friends' and were soon his favourite photographic subjects. As the children grew older, Dodgson took them out for boating expeditions on the river, entertaining them with songs, riddles and stories. On 4 July 1862 he improvized a story especially for Alice, in which she was the central character. At the end of the day, she asked him to write the story down for her. 'And so', Dodgson wrote many years later, 'to please a child I loved (I don't remember any other reason) I printed in manuscript, and illustrated with my own crude designs' the story of *Alice's Adventures Under Ground.*

By the time the book was completed, Dodgson was estranged from the Liddells. Mrs. Liddell destroyed all his letters to Alice and their friendship cooled. Meanwhile, he had been encouraged by his friends to publish the story, and in 1863 approached Alexander Macmillan with a view to having it brought out at his own expense. He added two important new episodes 'Pig and Pepper' and 'A Mad Tea-Party'. He was, however, all too well aware that his own fantastic, roughly-drawn illustrations would not be suitable for publication. Never a man for half-measures, he contacted the leading illustrator and political cartoonist of the day, John Tenniel, who agreed to undertake the commission.

Tenniel worked slowly and was constantly harassed by Dodgson's relentless and detailed criticism, but, after many vicissitudes, including the scrapping of the first edition, the newly-titled *Alice's Adventures in Wonderland* finally appeared in November 1865. It was totally unlike any other book for children; it drew no moral, it did not seek to instruct. Although the book sold slowly at first, the astonishing originality of Dodgson's imagination established the book as a classic that was as popular with adults as with children.

In Dodgson's lifetime it was translated into Danish, Dutch, French, German, Italian, Russian, Swedish and even into shorthand. In 1889 the author produced a version for children who were too young to read it for themselves, *The Nursery Alice.*

In 1867 Dodgson took his first and only trip abroad. His friend Henry Parry Liddon was setting out for Russia on a mission to establish closer relations between the churches of England and Russia and he suggested that Dodgson should go with him. They travelled by way of Brussels and Cologne where Dodgson was so overcome by the beauty of the cathedral that Liddon found him 'sobbing like a child'. He reacted to St. Petersburg with an almost childish delight 'the little *droshkies* that went running about, seemingly quite indifferent to running over anybody', and was highly pleased with himself when he got the better of a *droshkie* driver who tried to overcharge him. In Moscow he followed a performance of *Aladdin* with the help of a pocket dictionary. The return route took them through Warsaw and Paris where Dodgson took himself to the Opéra Comique while Liddon was having discussions on the Pan-Anglian Synod. It is not surprising that his companion found Dodgson rather frivolous at times.

Shortly after his return to England, Dodgson's father died and he found himself the head of a large family. One of his first tasks was to find a new home for his sisters and eventually Dodgson acquired 'The Chestnuts' in Guildford, Surrey. It was there, walking on the Downs while taking a break from nursing his sick godson, that the last line of *The Hunting of the Snark* came suddenly into his mind: 'For the Snark *was* a Boojum, you see'. Over the years, the rest of the poem slowly came together and it was eventually published in 1876. Dodgson always insisted that he had no idea what it meant.

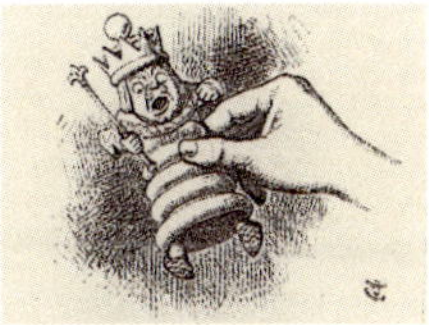

[Figure 10]
Sir John Tenniel's illustration of the White King from *Through the Looking-Glass and What Alice Found There*, 1872

As early as August 1866, Dodgson had told Macmillan that he had a 'floating idea of writing a sort of sequel to Alice'. Although he was now estranged from the Liddells, the stories and songs he had invented for the girls were still fresh in his memory, and these provided him with much of the material for *Through the Looking-Glass and What Alice Found There*. Tenniel was reluctant to work with Dodgson again but no other suitable illustrator could be found and he allowed himself to be persuaded. The book was published in December 1871. In contrast to the summer riverside setting of *Alice's Adventures*, *Through the Looking-Glass* proved to be a winter story with undertones of menace and decay. Nevertheless, there was enough high-spirited nonsense and fantasy to make the book as popular as its predecessor.

Dodgson had always been fascinated by the theatre and during vacations he would often see as many as three or four plays a week. Through his photography he became a friend of Ellen Terry, the most famous actress of her day (see plate page 54). He had ambitions to become a dramatist, but his only attempt at a play, a sentimental melodrama entitled *Morning Clouds*, never developed beyond an outline. While many of his contemporaries were scandalized at the notion of a clergyman being associated with the stage, Dodgson believed that it had a great potential for good and tried to promote a theatre for children. In 1886 the *Alice* books, which Dodgson had longed to see on the stage, were made into an operetta by Henry Savile Clarke and presented at the Prince of Wales' theatre.

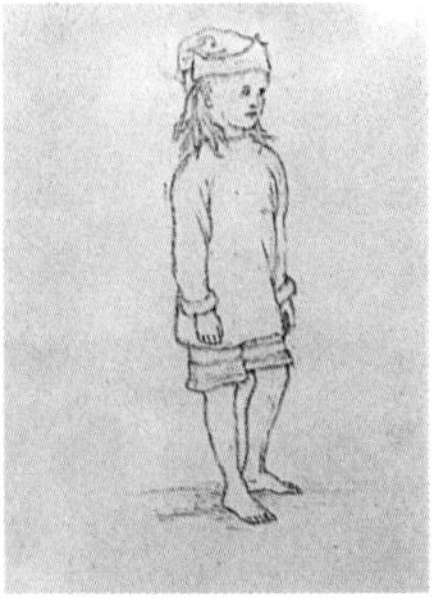

[Figure 11]
Lewis Carroll's drawing of Gertrude Chataway
Dodgson Family Collection, Surrey History Service

'Children are three-fourths of my life', Dodgson once informed a colleague, and Beatrice Hatch, who had first met him when she was under five, wrote, 'Never surely did any man make more friends among children than he did'. Although he had many friends, he was always happiest in the company of little girls. He would meet them on trains or at the seaside and share their world, entertaining them with games and puzzles. They unlocked the doors of his imagination and all his major works were dedicated to little girls. The majority of his child friendships came to an end at adolescence 'where the stream and river meet', but others survived into adult life, where Dodgson became a trusted friend, showing particular understanding for young women who set out to lead an independent life in teaching or in the theatre.

Dodgson had the kind of mind that could never entirely be at rest. When he could not sleep at night he kept his mind occupied with mathematical problems. He even contrived a 'nyctograph' so that he could write down ideas in the dark. Like the White Knight in *Through the Looking-Glass*, he was constantly inventing things – a copying machine, a London street finder, a form of Scrabble, a new kind of postal order. He devised schemes for proportional representation, judging lawn-tennis tournaments and betting on horses. Games held an irresistible fascination for him – word games like 'Doublets' and 'Mischmasch' and Carrollean sports – 'Castle Croquet' and 'Circular Billiards'. In his later years he was preoccupied with the study of logic. This too formed the basis of a popular game, but it had a deeper purpose, for he believed that an understanding of logic would help people to deal with religious difficulties.

In December 1867 Dodgson published in *Aunt Judy's Magazine* a fairy story entitled 'Bruno's Revenge'. The adventures of Bruno and his sister Sylvie were to engage Dodgson almost to the end of his life. For several years Lord Salisbury and his wife invited Dodgson to their New Year celebrations at Hatfield House, and it became the custom for him to tell a Sylvie and Bruno story to the children. Eventually he found that he had sufficient material for a full-length book and he set to work to devise a framework for the stories. In the end, the framework became so complex that it completely dominated the book and in his attempt to introduce into *The Story of Sylvie and Bruno* elements 'not wholly out of harmony with the graver cadences of life', the Reverend Charles Dodgson effectively stifled Lewis Carroll.

Dodgson died, suddenly and unexpectedly, of pneumonia, a few days before his sixty-sixth birthday on 14 January 1898 at his family home, 'The Chestnuts'. He is buried in Guildford Cemetery, but there is also a plaque to his memory in Poets' Corner, Westminster Abbey. The *Alice* books, which continue to fascinate readers throughout the world, are his true memorial.

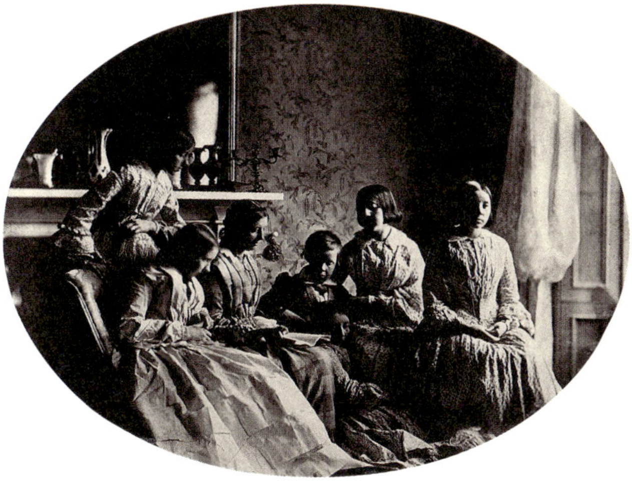

'The New Book', Six of Dodgson's sisters and brother, Edwin, 1857

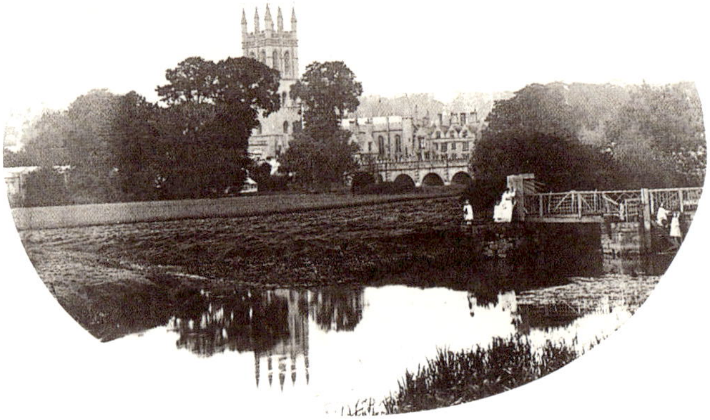

Magdalen Tower, Oxford, 1861

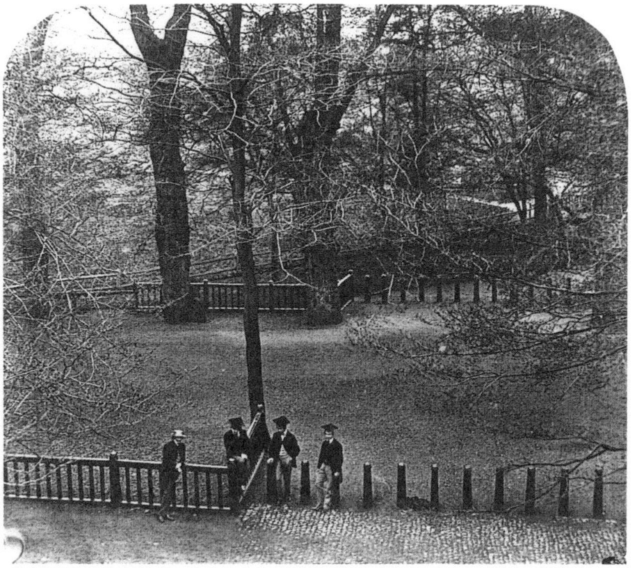

The Broad Walk, Oxford, 1857

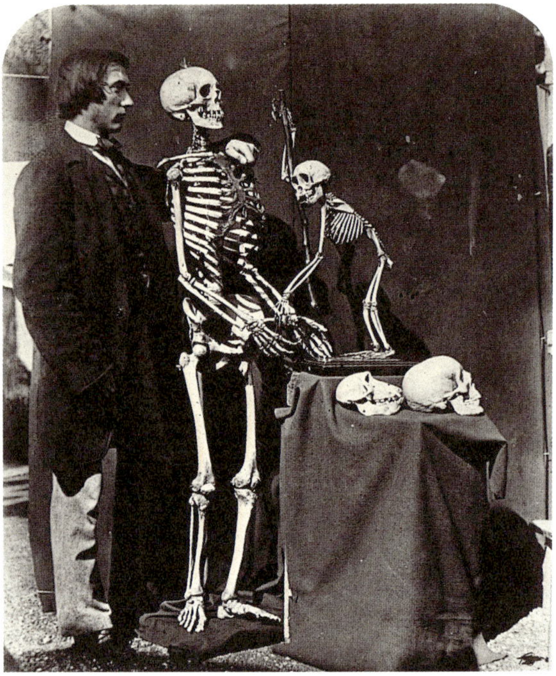

Reginald Southey with Skeletons and Skulls, 1857

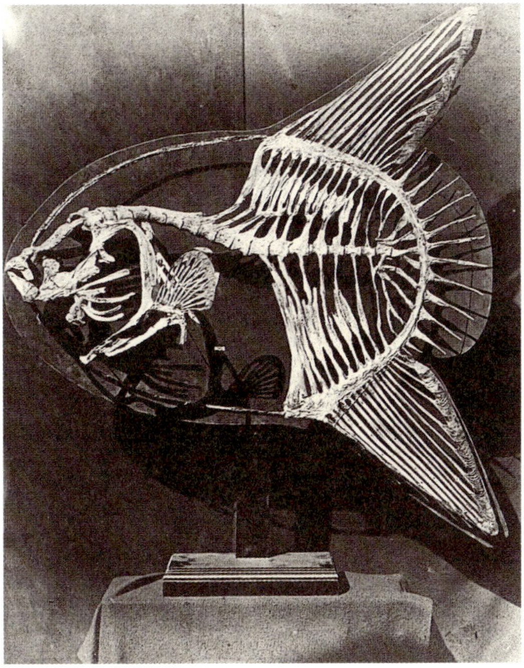

Skeleton of the Sun Fish, 1857

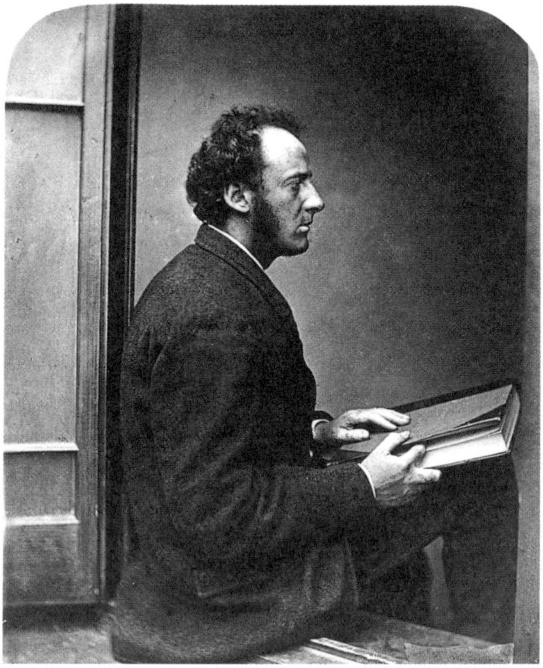

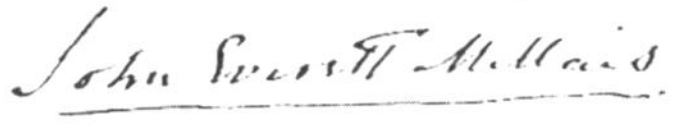

John Everett Millais, 1865

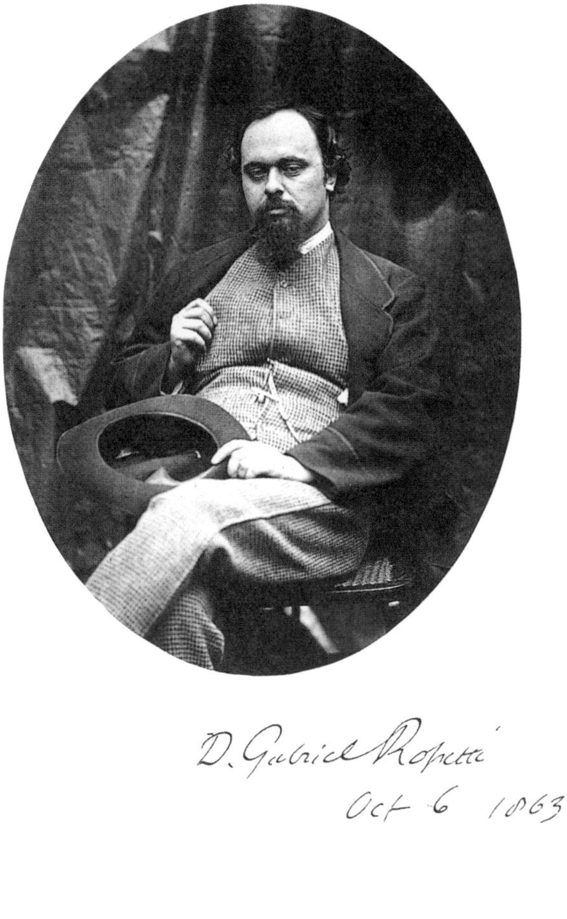

Dante Gabriel Rossetti, 1863

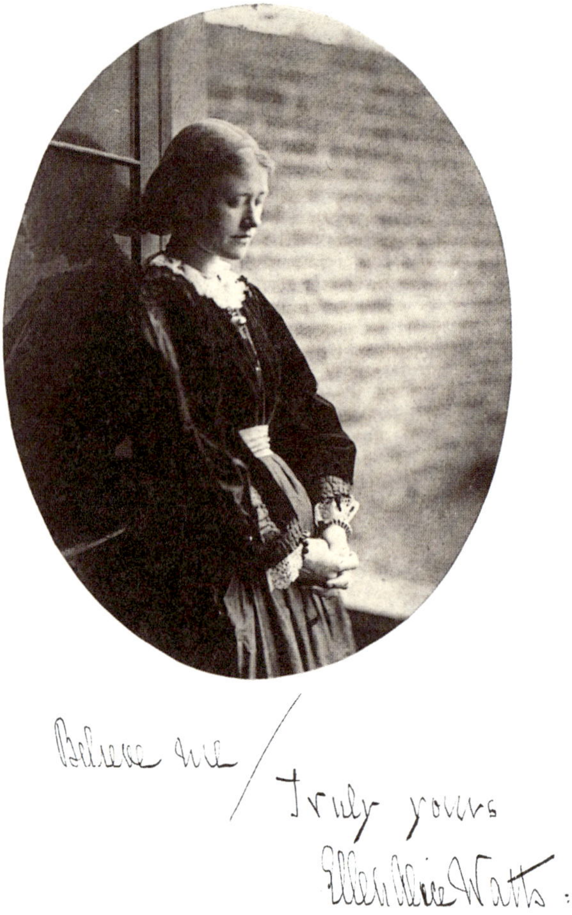

Ellen Alice Watts, née Terry, 1865

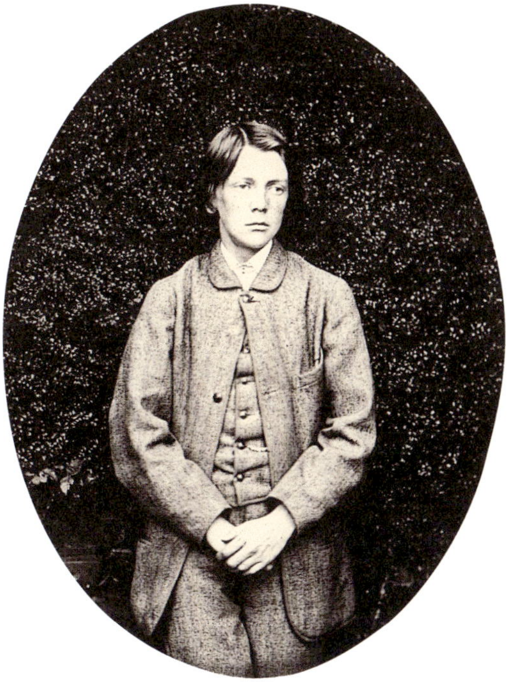

Aubrey Taylor, 1862

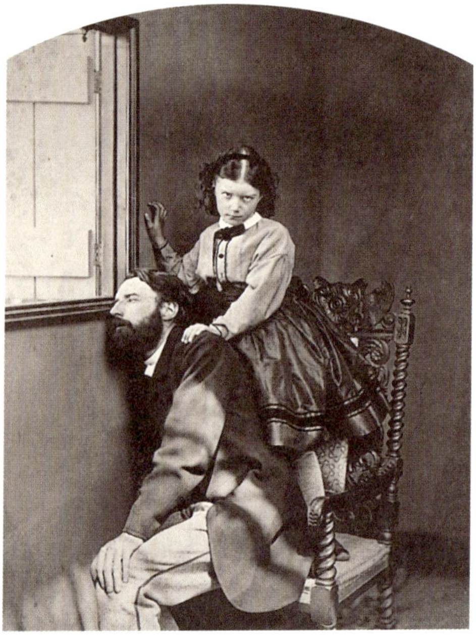

Reverend Thomas Childe Barker and May, 1864

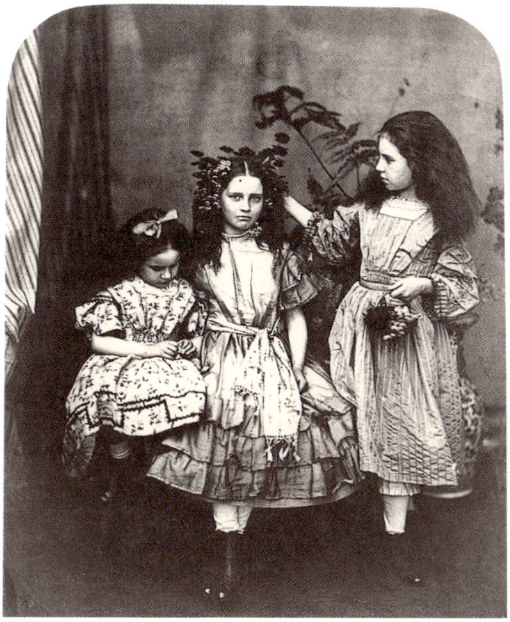

Irene MacDonald, Flo Rankin & Mary MacDonald, 1863

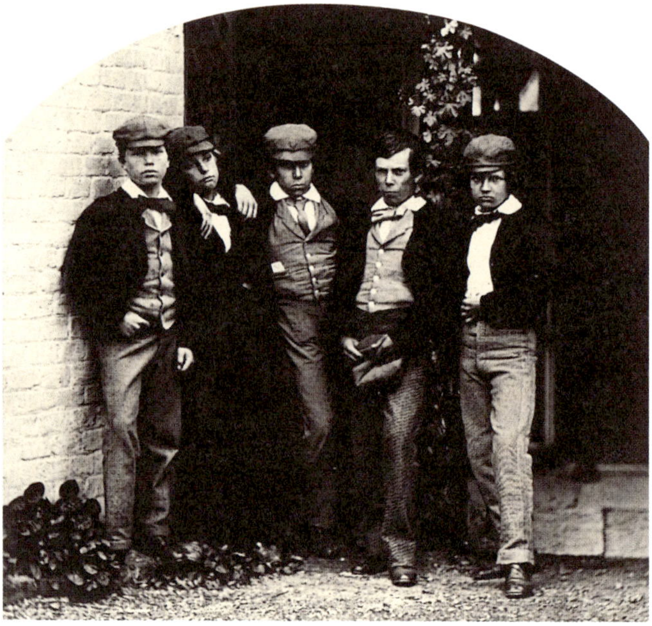

Clement De Malet
John Henry Clutton
Ralph Clutton
F. G. Richardson
John St J Frederick

Five boys from Twyford School, 1859

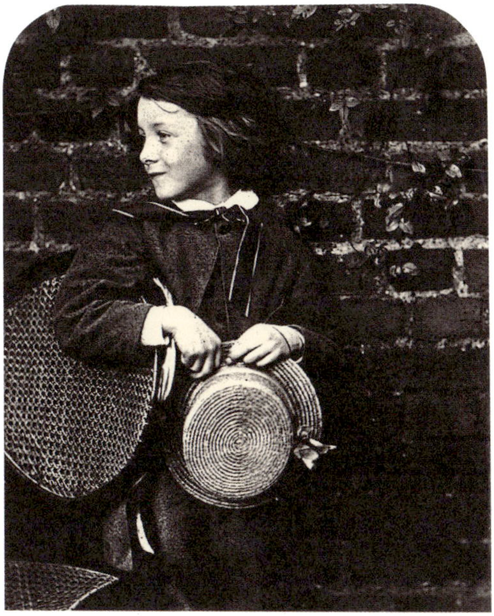

Arthur Hughes.

Arthur Hughes, 1863

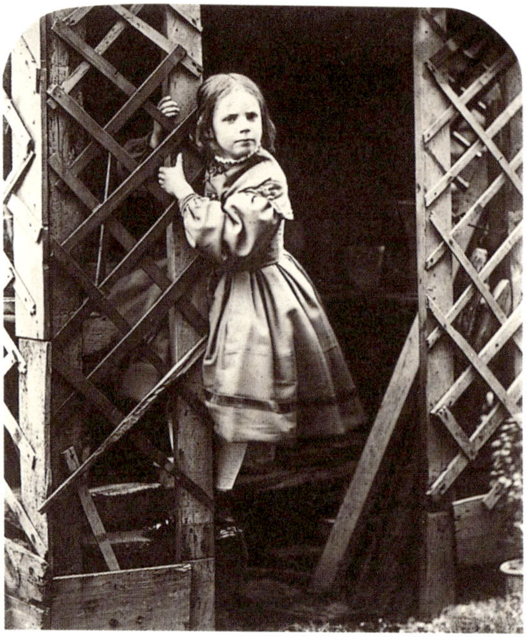

Louisa D. Barry, 1860

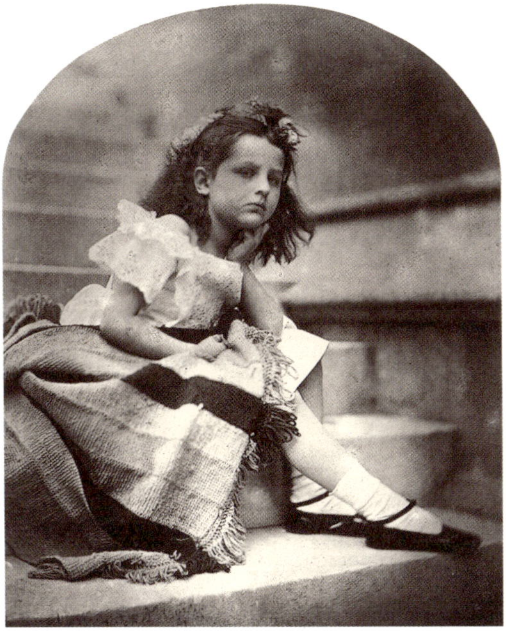

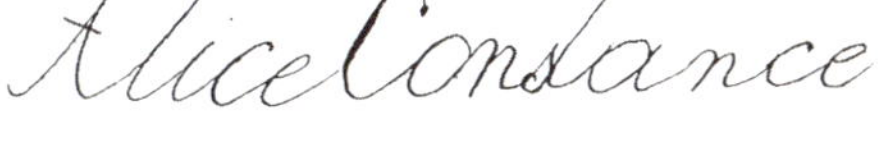

Alice Constance Westmacott, 1864

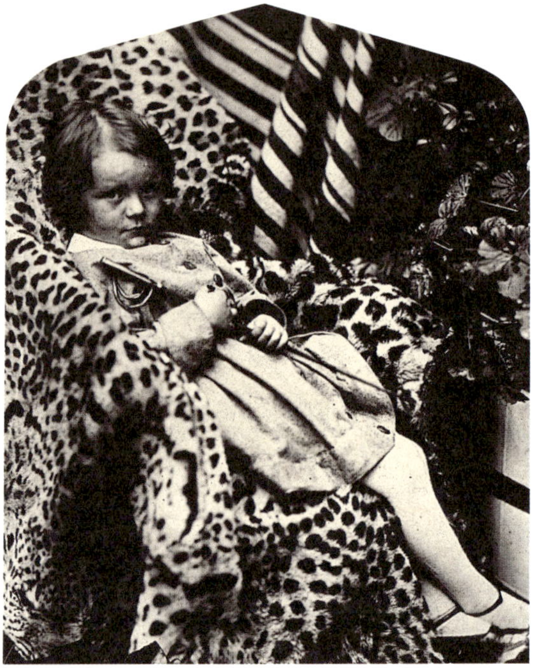

Wickliffe Taylor, 1863

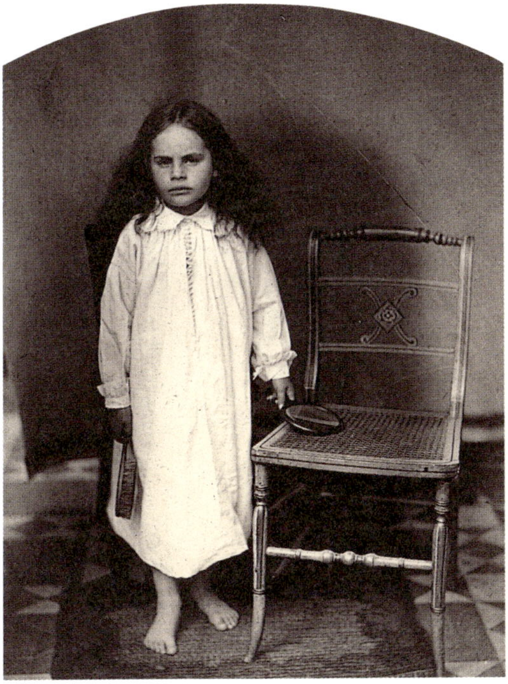

'It won't come smooth', Irene MacDonald, 1863

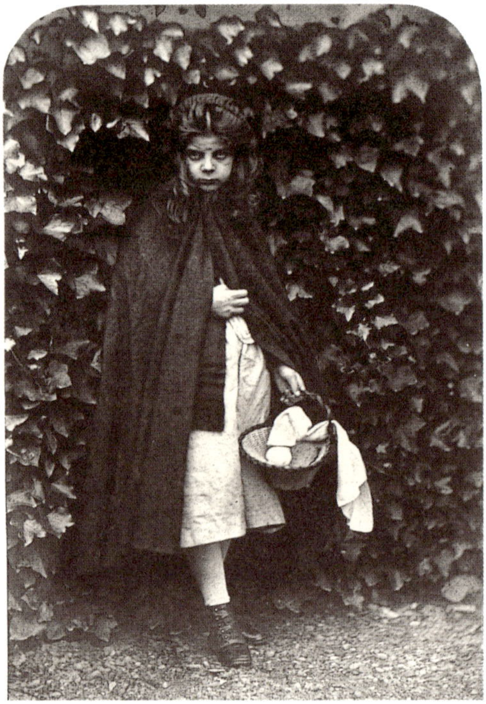

'Little Red Riding Hood', Agnes Grace Weld, 1857

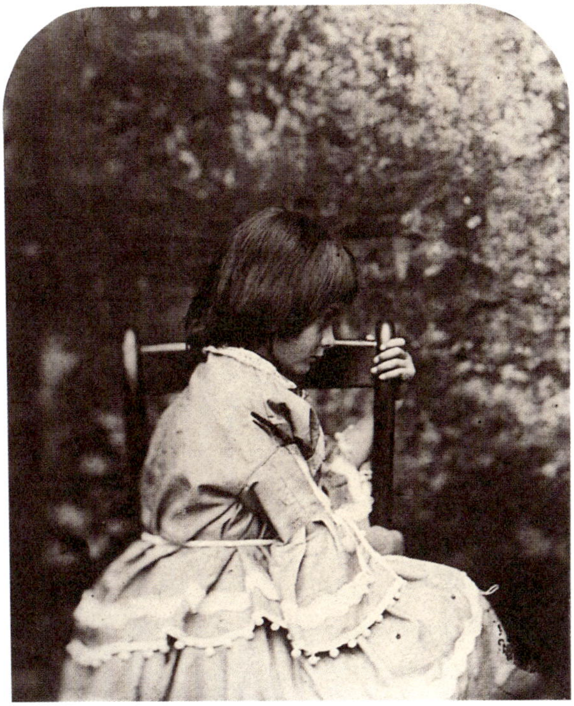

Alice Liddell, 1858

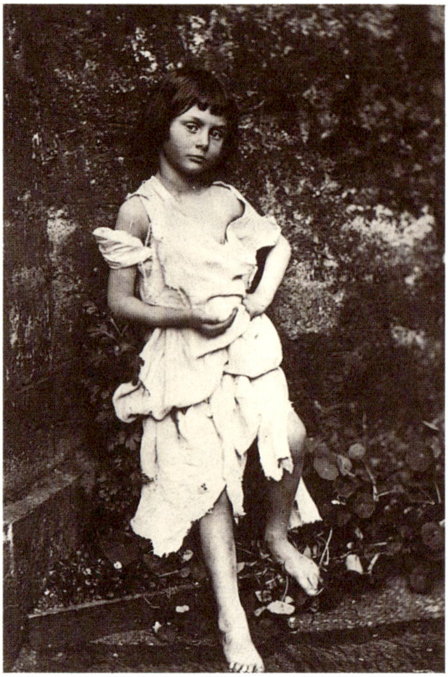

'A Beggar Maid', Alice Liddell, 1858

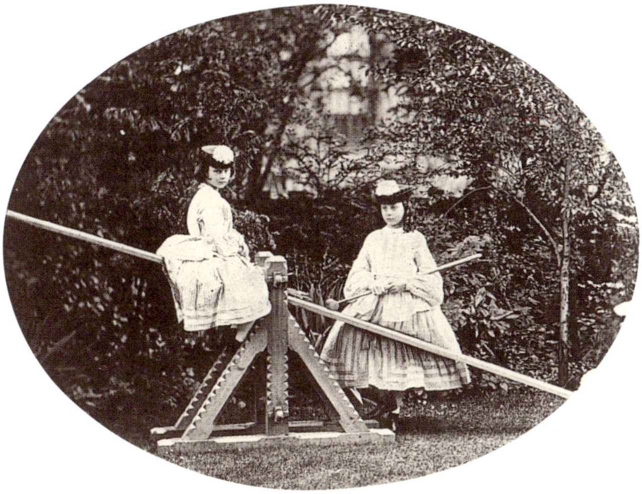

Alice and Lorina Liddell on a See-Saw, 1860

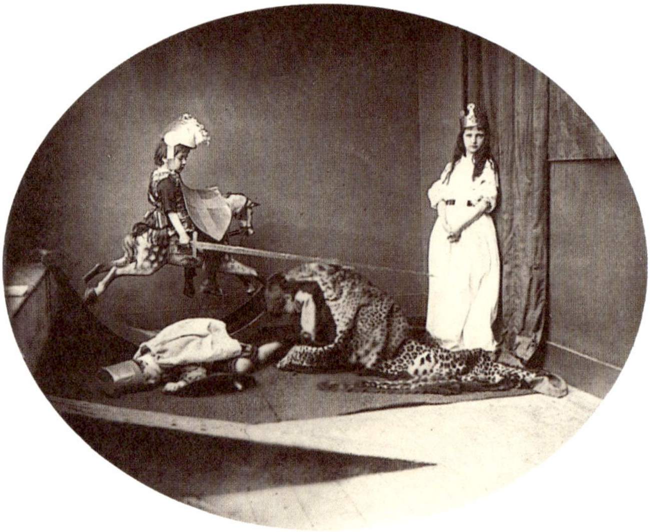

'St. George & The Dragon', Four Kitchin children, 1875

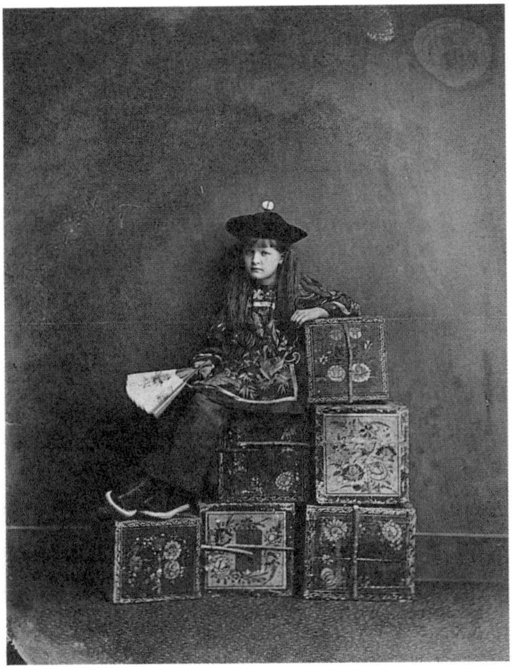

'A Tea Merchant', Xie Kitchin, 1873

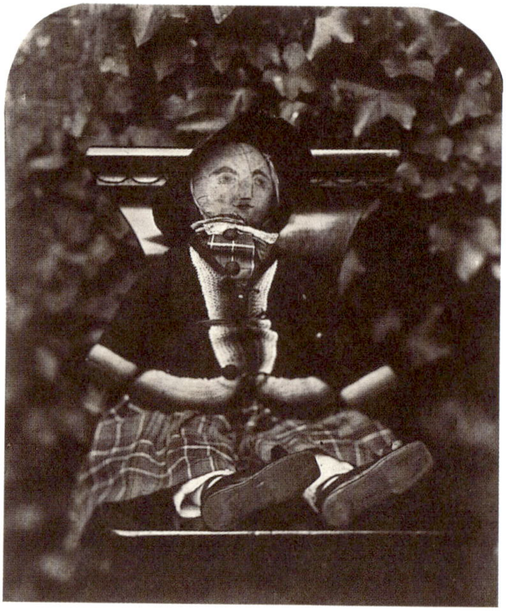

'Tim', The Dodgson's family doll, at Croft, 1858

The Complete works of Lewis Carroll
Penguin Books, 1997

Lewis Carroll: a biography
Morton N. Cohen, Macmillan, 1995

Lewis Carroll: a biography
Michael Bakewell, Heinemann, 1996

Lewis Carroll: interviews and recollections
ed. Morton N. Cohen, Macmillan, 1989

The Letters of Lewis Carroll
ed. Morton N. Cohen and
Roger Lancelyn Green,
Macmillan, 1979

Selected Letters of Lewis Carroll
ed. Morton N. Cohen, Macmillan, 1982

Looking-Glass Letters
selected by Thomas Hinde, Collins & Brown, 1991

Lewis Carroll, Photographer
Helmut Gernsheim, Dover, 1969

Lewis Carroll's Games and Puzzles
Edward Wakeling, Dover, 1992

The Diaries of Lewis Carroll
ed. Roger Lancelyn Green have long been out of print, but a new edition, edited by Edward Wakeling, is being issued by the Lewis Carroll Society.

Secret Gardens; a study of the Golden Age of children's literature
Humphrey Carpenter, Unwin, 1987

Some Versions of Pastoral
William Empson, Peregrine, 1966

Aspects of Alice
ed. Robin Phillips, Penguin, 1974

Inventing Wonderland
Jackie Wullschläger, Methuen, 1995

All dimensions are height x width in centimetres.

Lewis Carroll carefully assigned numbers to both his negatives and prints. The numbering of his prints is chronological and was applied consistently throughout his photographic career . It is the print numbers that are cited here in square brackets [ ]. Carroll's negative numbering sequence is much more complex to follow as he recycles the glass plates from old negatives, reassigning their numbers.

The prints in this exhibition have been produced on fine art paper by the Iris printing process, using inks which have a life expectancy of between 50 to 100 years.

THE DODGSON FAMILY AT CROFT RECTORY

1.
Charles Lutwidge Dodgson, 1857
9.1 x 5.7
By courtesy of the National Portrait Gallery, London

2.
Archdeacon Dodgson, 1856
18.0 x 11.5 [63]
Gernsheim Collection, Harry Ransom Humanities Research Center, The University of Texas at Austin

3.
Croft Rectory, 1856
15.0 x 15.5 [64]
Morris L. Parrish Collection, Department of Rare Books and Special Collections, Princeton University Library

4.
The Drawing Room, Croft Rectory, 1856
12.5 x 13.2
Gernsheim Collection, Harry Ransom Humanities Research Center, The University of Texas at Austin

5.
Wilfred Dodgson and Dido, 1857
14.0 x 11.5 [278]
Morris L. Parrish Collection, Department of Rare Books and Special Collections, Princeton University Library

6.
'The Reflection',
Margaret Dodgson, 1862
10.2 x 7.5 [897]
Morris L. Parrish Collection, Department of Rare Books and Special Collections, Princeton University Library

7.
Skeffington Hume Dodgson, 1856
13.7 x 10.5 [102]
Gernsheim Collection, Harry Ransom Humanities Research Center, The University of Texas at Austin

8.
'The New Book', Six of Dodgson's Sisters and Brother, Edwin, 1857
12.3 x 16.4 [248]
Gernsheim Collection, Harry Ransom Humanities Research Center, The University of Texas at Austin

9.
'Tim',
The Dodgson's family doll, at Croft, 1858
13.0 x 10.5 [344]
Morris L. Parrish Collection, Department of Rare Books and Special Collections, Princeton University Library

LIFE AT OXFORD UNIVERSITY

10.
Magdalen Tower, Oxford, 1861
14.0 x 18.0 [721]
Morris L. Parrish Collection, Department of Rare Books and Special Collections, Princeton University Library

11.
The Broad Walk, Oxford, 1857
13.3 x 17.2 [173]
Morris L. Parrish Collection, Department of Rare Books and Special Collections, Princeton University Library

12.
The Broad Walk, Oxford, 1857
15.0 x 16.5 [213]
Morris L. Parrish Collection, Department of Rare Books and Special Collections, Princeton University Library

13.
Dr. George Rolleston and students examining skeleton, 1857
15.0 x 17.0 [205]
Morris L. Parrish Collection, Department of Rare Books and Special Collections, Princeton University Library

14.
Reginald Southey with Skeletons and Skulls, 1857
16.7 x 13.8 [219]
National Museum of Photography, Film & Television, Bradford, United Kingdom (by courtesy of the Board of Trustees of the Science Museum)

15.
Skeleton of the Sun Fish, 1857
16.0 x 12.5 [215]
Morris L. Parrish Collection, Department of Rare Books and Special Collections, Princeton University Library

16.
Cod's Head and Shoulders and Human Skull, 1857
12.5 x 17.0 [210]
Morris L. Parrish Collection, Department of Rare Books and Special Collections, Princeton University Library

17.
Quintin Twiss in "The Two Bonnycastles", 1858
17.0 x 13.0 [352]
Morris L. Parrish Collection, Department of Rare Books and Special Collections, Princeton University Library

18.
Thomas Combe, Printer to the University, 1860
14.0 x 11.5 [606]
Morris L. Parrish Collection, Department of Rare Books and Special Collections, Princeton University Library

19.
Dr. Henry Parry Liddon, 1857
12.6 x 10.3 [228]
By courtesy of the National Portrait Gallery, London

20.
Thomas Vere Bayne, 1857
14.0 x 11.4 [181]
By courtesy of the National Portrait Gallery, London

21.
Lord Salisbury and his eldest two sons, Oxford, 1870
11.0 x 8.5 [1870]
Morris L. Parrish Collection, Department of Rare Books and Special Collections, Princeton University Library

FAMOUS SITTERS, FRIENDS AND RELATIONS

22.
Prince Leopold, 1875
17.8 x 12.7 [2305]
Gernsheim Collection, Harry Ransom Humanities Research Center, The University of Texas at Austin

23.
John Everett Millais, 1865
12.5 x 9.8 [1366]
Gernsheim Collection, Harry Ransom Humanities Research Center, The University of Texas at Austin

24.
The Four Rossettis, 1863
16.4 x 20.2 [1132]
Gernsheim Collection, Harry Ransom Humanities Research Center, The University of Texas at Austin

25.
Dante Gabriel Rossetti, 1863
14.3 x 19.0 [1126]
Gernsheim Collection, Harry Ransom Humanities Research Center, The University of Texas at Austin

26.
William Holman Hunt, 1860
17.5 x 13.0 [576]
Morris L. Parrish Collection, Department of Rare Books and Special Collections, Princeton University Library

27.
Thomas Woolner, 1860
17.0 x 13.0 [584]
Morris L. Parrish Collection, Department of Rare Books and Special Collections, Princeton University Library

28.
Alexander Munro and Wife, 1863
13.8 x 11.4 [1136]
Gernsheim Collection, Harry Ransom Humanities Research Center, The University of Texas at Austin

29.
Arthur Hughes and Daughter, 1863
20.4 x 15.2 [1177]
Gernsheim Collection, Harry Ransom Humanities Research Center, The University of Texas at Austin

30.
John Ruskin, 1875
10.0 circular [2309]
Morris L. Parrish Collection, Department of Rare Books and Special Collections, Princeton University Library

31.
Professor Michael Faraday, 1860
14.0 x 10.0 [574]
Morris L. Parrish Collection, Department of Rare Books and Special Collections, Princeton University Library

32.
John Phillips, 1866
12.6 x 9.5 [1501]
Gernsheim Collection, Harry Ransom Humanities Research Center, The University of Texas at Austin

33.
Sir Roderick Impey Murchison, 1860
14.0 x 10.5 [596]
Morris L. Parrish Collection, Department of Rare Books and Special Collections, Princeton University Library

34.
George and Lily Scott MacDonald, 1863
20.6 x 15.3 [1183]
Gernsheim Collection, Harry Ransom Humanities Research Center, The University of Texas at Austin

35.
Reverend Thomas Childe Barker and May, 1864
20.4 x 15.3 [1233]
Gernsheim Collection, Harry Ransom Humanities Research Center, The University of Texas at Austin

36.
Reverend R. Gandell and Florence, 1862
12.0 x 16.0 [769]
Morris L. Parrish Collection, Department of Rare Books and Special Collections, Princeton University Library

37.
Tom Taylor, 1863
20.4 x 15.3 [1111]
Gernsheim Collection, Harry Ransom Humanities Research Center, The University of Texas at Austin

38.
Charlotte and Frances Yonge, 1866
12.9 x 10.1 [1453]
Gernsheim Collection, Harry Ransom Humanities Research Center, The University of Texas at Austin

39.
Wilfred Dodgson on his 'Boneshaker' velocipede, 1869
18.4 x 15.2 [1754]
Gernsheim Collection, Harry Ransom Humanities Research Center, The University of Texas at Austin

40.
Charlotte Mary Dodgson, 1862
13.0 x 10.0 [850]
Morris L. Parrish Collection, Department of Rare Books and Special Collections, Princeton University Library

41.
Miss Cole, 1859
13.0 x 11.0 [454]
Morris L. Parrish Collection, Department of Rare Books and Special Collections, Princeton University Library

42.
Ellen Alice Watts, née Terry, 1865
8.8 x 6.5 [1330]
Gernsheim Collection, Harry Ransom Humanities Research Center, The University of Texas at Austin

43.
Mrs. Watts and Florence, 1865
10.0 x 7.6 [1331]
Gernsheim Collection, Harry Ransom Humanities Research Center, The University of Texas at Austin

44.
Henry Taylor, 1862
21.0 x 15.0 [881]
Morris L. Parrish Collection, Department of Rare Books and Special Collections, Princeton University Library

45.
J. Marshall and Julia, 1857
14.0 x 11.5 [308]
Morris L. Parrish Collection, Department of Rare Books and Special Collections, Princeton University Library

46.
The Tennyson and Marshall Families, 1857
13.0 x 14.0 [310]
Morris L. Parrish Collection, Department of Rare Books and Special Collections, Princeton University Library

47.
Alfred, Lord Tennyson, 1857
22.3 x 17.6 [306]
Gernsheim Collection, Harry Ransom Humanities Research Center, The University of Texas at Austin

'CHILD – FRIENDS'

48.
Alice Liddell, 1858
13.00 x 10.5 [355]
Morris L. Parrish Collection, Department of Rare Books and Special Collections, Princeton University Library

49.
Alice Liddell, 1860
14.0 x 11.5 [613]
Morris L. Parrish Collection, Department of Rare Books and Special Collections, Princeton University Library

50.
Alice and Lorina Liddell on a See-Saw, 1860
12.0 x 16.0 [563]
Morris L. Parrish Collection, Department of Rare Books and Special Collections, Princeton University Library

51.
'A Beggar Maid',
Alice Liddell, 1858
16.2 x 10.7 [354]
The Gilman Paper Company Collection

52.
'Waking',
Mary Millais, 1865
12.4 x 10.0 [1369]
Gernsheim Collection, Harry Ransom Humanities Research Center, The University of Texas at Austin

53.
Amy Hughes, 1863
12.5 x 9.9 [1172]
Gernsheim Collection, Harry Ransom Humanities Research Center, The University of Texas at Austin

54.
Arthur Hughes, jnr. 1863
12.5 x 9.9 [1171]
Gernsheim Collection, Harry Ransom Humanities Research Center, The University of Texas at Austin

55.
Louisa D. Barry, 1860
14.0 x 11.5 [622]
Morris L. Parrish Collection, Department of Rare Books and Special Collections, Princeton University Library

56.
Kathleen Tidy, 1858
13.5 x 9.0 [341]
Morris L. Parrish Collection, Department of Rare Books and Special Collections, Princeton University Library

57.
'No Lessons Today',
Flora Rankin, 1863
16.5 x 13.0 [1017]
Morris L. Parrish Collection, Department of Rare Books and Special Collections, Princeton University Library

58.
Wickliffe Taylor, 1863
12.6 x 10.3 [1116]
Gernsheim Collection, Harry Ransom Humanities Research Center, The University of Texas at Austin

59.
Hallam Tennyson, 1857
14.0 x 11.5 [305]
Morris L. Parrish Collection, Department of Rare Books and Special Collections, Princeton University Library

60.
Clement D. E. Malet, 1859
13.0 x 10.5 [400]
Morris L. Parrish Collection, Department of Rare Books and Special Collections, Princeton University Library

61.
Aubrey Taylor, 1862
14.0 x 10.0 [876]
Morris L. Parrish Collection, Department of Rare Books and Special Collections, Princeton University Library

62.
Five boys fromTwyford School, 1859
14.0 x 14.5 [392]
Morris L. Parrish Collection, Department of Rare Books and Special Collections, Princeton University Library

63.
Gertrude Dykes, 1862
21.0 x 15.0 [904]
Morris L. Parrish Collection, Department of Rare Books and Special Collections, Princeton University Library

64.
Alice Constance Westmacott, 1864
12.6 x 9.9 [1316]
Gernsheim Collection, Harry Ransom Humanities Research Center, The University of Texas at Austin

65.
Marion 'Polly' & Florence Terry, 1865
12.6 x 9.5 [1341]
Gernsheim Collection, Harry Ransom Humanities Research Center, The University of Texas at Austin

66.
'It won't come smooth',
Irene MacDonald, 1863
20.5 x 15.3 [1027]
Gernsheim Collection, Harry Ransom Humanities Research Center, The University of Texas at Austin

67.
'St. George & The Dragon',
Four Kitchin Children, 1875
10.7 x 14.1 [2316]
The Gilman Paper Company Collection

68.
'Little Red Riding Hood',
Agnes Grace Weld, 1857
14.2 x 9.7 [275]
Gernsheim Collection, Harry Ransom Humanities Research Center, The University of Texas at Austin

69.
'A Tea Merchant',
Xie Kitchin 1873
19.0 x 14.7 [2155]
Gernsheim Collection, Harry Ransom Humanities Research Center, The University of Texas at Austin

70.
Xie Kitchin with Parasol, 1876
12.6 x 15.5 [2422]
Gernsheim Collection, Harry Ransom Humanities Research Center, The University of Texas at Austin

71.
'Rosy Dreams and Slumbers Light',
Xie Kitchin, 1873
12.6 x 15.6 [2153]
Gernsheim Collection, Harry Ransom Humanities Research Center, The University of Texas at Austin

72.
Irene MacDonald, Flo Rankin & Mary MacDonald, 1863
22.2 x 18.0
The Gilman Paper Company Collection

73.
Irene MacDonald, laid on Rugs, 1863
14.2 x 19.0 [1008]
Gernsheim Collection, Harry Ransom Humanities Research Centre, The University of Texas at Austin

74.
Charlotte & Mary Webster, and Margaret Gatey, 1857
8.6 x 16.3 [300]
National Museum of Photography, Film & Television, Bradford, United Kingdom (by courtesy of the Board of Trustees of the Science Museum).

75.
Evelyn Hatch, reclining nude, 1879
11.0 x 16.0
Courtesy the Rosenbach Museum & Library, Philadelphia, PA

76.
Evelyn Hatch on a River Bank, 1879
22.1 x 16.7
Courtesy the Rosenbach Museum & Library, Philadelphia, PA

77.
Annie & Frances Henderson as Castaways, 1879
15.0 x 12.2
Courtesy the Rosenbach Museum & Library, Philadelphia, PA

ILLUSTRATIONS COPYRIGHT